To Daniel Greenberg:
who has transformed school into
a learning center, rather than a
teaching center.

Russ Ackoff

8 . 1 . 03 .

Redesigning Society

REDESIGNING SOCIETY

Russell L. Ackoff

Sheldon Rovin

STANFORD BUSINESS BOOKS
An imprint of Stanford University Press

Stanford University Press
Stanford, California

Library of Congress Cataloging-in-Publication Data

Ackoff, Russell Lincoln, 1919–
   Redesigning society / Russell L. Ackoff, Sheldon Rovin
     p. cm.
   Includes bibliographical references and index.
   ISBN 0-8047-4794-6 (alk. paper)
    1. Social problems—United States.   2. Social change—United States.
3. United States—Social policy—1993– I. Rovin, Sheldon. II. Title.
HN59.2.A26 2003
361.1'0973—dc21   2003007386

Printed in the United States of America on acid-free, archival-quality paper.

Original printing 2003

The last figure below indicates the year of this printing:
12 11 10 09 08 07 06 05 04 03

Designed and typeset at Stanford University Press in 10/13.5 Sabon.

To Ray Stata,
friend and patron

Contents

List of Illustrations   ix

Preface   xi

1 Society and Its Design   1

2 Governance   14

3 The City, Housing, and Transport   39

4 Health Care   62

5 Education   82

6 Welfare   110

7 Crime and Punishment   124

8 Leading Development   150

Epilogue: How to Get Started   165

Appendix: A Way of Resolving Conflict   167

References   171

Index   173

Illustrations

2.1   A Part of the Structure of Government   23

2.2   Possible Errors on the Issue of Capital Punishment   31

3.1   The Conceptual (Fractal) City   45

3.2   A Schematic Block Design   47

3.3   Another Schematic Block Design   48

3.4   Two Alternative City Designs   50

3.5   A Schematic Design of an Urmobile   57

4.1   An Overview of the System   75

4.2   The Health Care Mall   79

5.1   An Arrangement of Computers to Facilitate Learning   89

5.2   A Basic Enclosed Unit in a University   107

5.3   A Trimester School Schedule   108

Preface

The serious or complex problems we face cannot be solved by the same consciousness that created them.

Albert Einstein

Societies, ours included, can and urgently need to be improved. Despite an abundance of food and appropriate health care, millions suffer from hunger and curable diseases. The United States is the only industrialized society without universal health care (Chapter 4). Education (Chapter 5) in the United States is in a sorry state with illiteracy being common. Despite increasing expenditures, efforts to improve education thus far have not borne fruit. Even in some well-developed countries, unemployment and the growing underclass present serious, intransigent problems—for example, "inherited poverty" or a permanent "welfare society" (Chapter 6).

Neighbor slaughters neighbor in the name of religion, race, ethnicity, nationalism, and sex. More people are in prison in the United States than are attending universities. Terrorism, crime, and violence are rampant, and corporate crime is wreaking havoc with the financial well-being of millions of U.S. citizens (Chapter 7).

Because of mini-wars, insurrections, and "policing actions," defense spending continues to dominate national budgets and as a result diverts resources that could be used for societal improvement. The maldistribution of wealth is increasing within and between most nations. The long-run ability of the environment to sustain life appears to be seriously threatened as pollution of air, water, and land increases and radioactive and other waste wait for discovery of an effective means of disposal. Deterioration of cities is the rule; in the center of many of the large cities it takes less time to walk from one point to another than to drive (Chapter 3). Few of the less-developed countries are on a path to development (Chapter 8); most continue to deteriorate. The quality of life and standard of living even in some of the more developed countries are decreasing. In many societies alienation is increasing. Throughout the world more and more people feel that they have no say in the governance of their society (Chapter 2). In the United States, this is reflected in the fact that less than half of those eligible vote in elections.

Despite all this, doomsday is not here and is not even imminent. Our intention is not to make a doom-and-gloom pronouncement, but to call attention to what can be done about societal problems by offering a redesign of society. A better society is possible, and we ought to be pursuing it intelligently.

We believe the problems described are universal and the designs we offer are applicable in some form to most societies.

The designs that follow in this book came from using the process of idealized design which is described in Chapter 1. It is a highly creative process because, as we will explain, it eliminates all but a few minor constraints and focuses on *what is wanted now*, not on what is not wanted or what is wanted in some distant future. It is only through creative thought and innovation that society can be transformed into one that provides a more equitable distribution of wealth, quality of life, and opportunities for development.

The concepts "right" and "wrong" and "true" and "false" are not applicable to a design, but one can like or dislike a design to varying degrees. Therefore, the concept of proof is not relevant; preference is. A design must be evaluated by the values of what it makes possible and what it makes impossible. However, not all the consequences of a design are apparent. The consequences are assumed by different people; hence their evaluations are likely to be different. We know this because many of the designs presented here differ significantly from the version that appeared in the first draft of this manuscript. Furthermore, evaluation of a design is also a matter of taste, and taste is a matter of aesthetics; *de gustibus non disputandum*: concerning taste there is no disputing.

It is our intent to stimulate thought and generate discussion and debate about the ideas and designs in this book. Through this publication we solicit suggestions from any and all who wish to make them. We will subsequently take their concepts, ideas, and design elements and improvement of our designs into account *as we continue to develop these designs*. In addition, we hope that others will take on continuation of the idealized design process and that such involvement will become widespread.

In the best of possible worlds this would lead to irresistible public pressure for progressive change.

We are very grateful for the comments and suggestions made by Herbert J. Addison, Kenneth MacLeod, Sandra Waddock, Kate Wahl, Mary Ray Worley, and Tony Hicks in particular, and the many others whose ideas have stimulated ours. We also want to acknowledge the contributions of Omid Nadoushani, who provided major input in the section on homelessness in Chapter 6.

Communications should be addressed to:

Russell L. Ackoff or Sheldon Rovin
1021 Lancaster Ave., Suite 201
Bryn Mawr, PA 19010
Phone: (610) 526–9374
Fax: (610) 526–9375
e-mail: rlackoff@aol.com

Redesigning Society

1   Society and Its Design

Large systems usually operate in failure mode. The system tends to oppose its own proper function.

John Gall

The thinking we use to redesign society stems from three essential concepts: doing the right thing, focusing on what we want, and thinking systemically.

First, Peter Drucker (1974) made a distinction between doing things right (efficiency) and doing the right thing (effectiveness). This is an incredibly important distinction that is not given enough attention in public affairs. The righter we do the wrong thing, the wronger we become. When a mistake is made doing the wrong thing and is corrected, we become wronger. In contrast, when a correction is made to an error in pursuing the right thing, we become better because we learn. It is far better to do the right thing wrong than to do the wrong thing right.

An example of doing the wrong thing right is the constant improvement of the automobile. Our automobiles are becoming faster even in the face of more urban congestion; they are becoming roomier even when the average occupancy of a driven automobile is fewer than two persons; and they are becoming bigger with the concomitant increase in fuel consumption even with their known contribution to environment pollution.

As we will show, most of our intransigent social problems—for example, crime and terrorism, deteriorating education, inadequate health care, and poverty—are consequences of doing the wrong things.

Second, most attempts to address societal problems are acts of desperation or political expediency. They focus on what is perceived to be wrong, deficiencies. Most current efforts to improve society are directed at getting rid of what we do *not* want rather than getting what we *do* want.

Getting rid of what we do not want often results in getting something worse. For example, when the United States tried to eliminate alcoholism by making alcoholic beverages illegal, it did not get rid of either alcoholism or alcohol, but it got a much worse problem, organized crime. Similarly, building more prisons to reduce crime exacerbates it, because incarceration currently increases both the likelihood of criminals committing crimes and the seriousness of the crimes they commit after they are released (Chapter 7). And making property taxes proportional to the value of a property encourages property deterioration and urban blight, since they reduce taxes.

A homely example of getting rid of something and then getting something worse occurs when we turn on a television set and get a program we do not want, which is most of the time. It is easy to get rid of an undesirable program by changing channels, but it is commonplace to get a program that we want even less. Such experiences reinforce the following principle:

> *Improvement of an existing condition or state requires a clear vision of what is wanted, not a clear vision of what is not wanted.*

Third, piecemeal improvements—improvement of different aspects of a society taken *separately*—are not likely to improve the properties and performance of society as a whole. A society is a system, and a system is understood by considering the whole, not the parts separately. Unfortunately, an insufficient number of those who govern or influence a society understand it and its implications for management, organization, or planning.

From Analysis to Synthesis: A New Way of Thinking

In the western part of the world, following Descartes, Newton, and the Renaissance, the universe has generally been believed to be a mechanism—a hermetically sealed clock—that was created by God to do his work. A clock is a mechanism that operates with a regularity dictated by its internal structure and the causal laws of nature, which Newton and his numerous followers believed he had formulated. Because of these beliefs, the universe was taken to be ultimately understandable, and such understanding was thought to be eventually obtainable by use of analysis. Analysis became the methodology of science and even became synonymous with ordinary thought. It is a three-set process: (1) take the thing or event to be understood apart; (2) explain the behavior or properties of the parts taken separately; and (3) aggregate the explanations of the parts into an understanding of the whole, the thing to explained.

The application of analysis gave rise to a critical question: Since most parts can themselves be taken apart, is there any end to this process? It followed from the belief that the universe was ultimately understandable that there had to be an end to the analytic reduction of parts—that is, that there were ultimate indivisible parts, elements. Analytically based science became a crusade in which the holy grail was the element; for example, atoms, particles, chemical elements (oxygen, carbon, hydrogen, etc.), cells, genes, instincts, and phonemes.

It is not surprising that humankind, believed to have been created in the image of God, should imitate his effort and create machines to do his *work*. Work was defined as the application of energy to matter so as to change matter's properties. Therefore, moving something, breaking it, or putting it together was taken to be work. The mechanization of work became the Industrial Revolution. In this revolution, machines came to serve the functions previously fulfilled by people and other animals, replacing the power of their muscles.

Over time a number of problems arose that could not be solved using this mechanistic view of the world. For example, the indeterminacy principle in physics, which asserts that it is impossible to know both the position and the momentum of a particle at a moment in time, put an end to the belief that the universe could be completely understood. Complete understanding came to be thought of as an approachable but unattainable ideal. Moreover, the focus on systems that emerged in the 1950s revealed the principal shortcoming of analytical thinking. As will be explained more fully in the next section, a system is a whole that is defined by its function in one or more larger systems of which it is a part. It cannot be divided into independent parts; its behavior and properties depend on how its parts *interact*, not on how they act taken separately. Therefore when a system is taken apart, it loses all of its essential properties and its ability to display its defining behavior, and so do its parts. For example, a disassembled automobile cannot carry people from one place to another, and the motor removed from the car cannot move anything, even itself.

Awareness of the nature of a system made it apparent that analysis of a system revealed its structure and how it worked, but not *why* it worked the way it does. In other words, analysis of systems was recognized as yielding only knowledge of systems, but not understanding of them. A new approach, *synthetic thinking*, was required to explain, to understand, systems.

Synthetic thinking is also a three-step process, each the opposite of the corresponding step of analysis: (1) identify one or more systems that contain the system to be explained; (2) explain the behavior of the containing system (or systems); and (3) disaggregate the understanding of the containing system into the role or function of the system to be explained. For example, an automobile is defined by its function in the transportation system: to carry people and goods from one place of their choosing to another, also of their choosing, under their control and in privacy.

While analysis reveals the structure of a system and how it works, synthetic thinking reveals why it behaves as it does. (No amount of analysis will reveal why the British drive on the "wrong" side of the street.) Systems thinking involves the use of both, analytic and synthetic thinking. The epitome of systems thinking is found in design; the epitome of analytic thinking is found in scientific research. Effective design requires the fusion of science, the arts, and the humanities.

Systems

A system (hence society) is a whole that has one or more defining functions and consists of two or more essential parts that satisfy three conditions.

In terms of its defining functions, every system (and, therefore, society) is defined by the function (or functions) it performs in one or more larger systems of which it is part and the function (or functions) it performs for its parts. For example, a computer is defined by what it does for those who use it—computation, word processing, communication—not by what it is made of. The functions of society involve meeting certain needs of its members—for example, providing water and transportation—and certain needs of the larger social system of which it is a part. Cities, for example, have obligations to states, states to nations, and nations to the United Nations or similar organizations.

> *The first of the three conditions that must be satisfied by an essential part of a system is that the system cannot do without the part to perform its defining function.*

A motor is an essential part of an automobile, but a cigarette lighter isn't. An automobile can transport people without a lighter but not without a motor. Similarly, the heart, lungs, and brain are among the essential parts of a person because without them a person cannot function or even live. The appendix is not an essential part of the body; it is added on, or attached, to the body. If the appendix is found to have a function, its name will have to be changed. In a society, government is an essential part, as are a police force and a justice system.

> *The second condition is that no essential part of a system can affect the system independently; how it affects the system as a whole depends on its interaction with at least one other essential part of the system.*

The essential parts are connected—that is, they interact—and they have interdependent effects on the whole. For example, the way a motor affects the performance of an automobile depends on the performance of at least the fuel pump and the battery. The way the heart affects the human body depends on what the brain and lungs are doing, and the way the brain affects the body depends on what the heart and lungs are doing, and so on. As we will see, without an understanding of the interactions of the essential parts of society, we cannot know how best to improve it.

> *The third condition is that no subsystem of a system— group of its essential parts—has an independent effect on the whole.*

For example, the fuel, electrical, and cooling subsystems of an automobile and the metabolic, motor, nervous, and circulatory subsystems of an organism do not have independent effects on the wholes of which they are parts. The same is true of the health, education, welfare, and criminal justice systems within society. They interact as do their individual parts. For example, a welfare system cannot succeed without some interactions with the education and health care systems.

In brief, then, each essential part or subsystem of a system has a (defining) function in that system that cannot be carried out independently of other parts. This means that the functioning of the part cannot be explained or understood apart from its interaction with the other parts.

> *When a system as a whole is divided into independent parts or subsystems, both the system and the parts lose their essential properties.*

Continuing the previous example, when the health care system is considered separately from education and welfare—as is usually the case—significant distortion of these parts occurs and the system as a whole is compromised and forced to function suboptimally.

SYSTEM PERFORMANCE

Obviously, the failure of any essential part of a system can result in the failure of that system, but when all essential parts are functioning properly, the system will also be functioning properly. Nevertheless, improving one or more parts may not serve to improve the whole.

> *Improvement in the performance of all or some part of a system taken separately may not, and often does not, improve the performance of the system as a whole; in fact, such improvements may destroy the system.*

Put another way, a system may not be the best available even when each of its parts is considered to be the best available. For example, suppose we determine which of the many available automobiles has the best motor, which the best transmission, which the best braking system, and so on for every essential part of an automobile. Then we remove these parts from their respective automobiles and try to assemble them into one automobile consisting only of the best available essential parts. We would not get the best automobile; in fact, we would not even get an automobile, because the parts would not fit together. Similarly, the best health, education, and welfare systems may not combine to make the best society. The performance of society as a whole depends more on how the parts, the subsystems, interact than on how they act separately. The construction of presumably better hospitals in the United States has not reduced the number of people with no health care coverage. In fact, this number has been increasing.

This implies that no part of a society should be designed independently of the other parts with which it will interact and without considering their joint effects on the performance of the whole. The properties designed into the parts should be derived from the properties desired of the society as a whole and the ways they must interact with other parts of the society. This principle explains why attempts to fix a serious social problem such as crime by dealing with only one of its aspects, incarceration of criminals, does not work. To reduce crime significantly, consideration must be given to other aspects of society such as education, employment, quality of life, segregation, discrimination, and the way justice is dispensed.

The defining properties of a system are properties of the whole that none of its parts has.

When architects design a house, they begin with a sketch of the whole, not of each room. Then they design the rooms to fit into that whole. If they see a way to improve a room, as they often do, they consider whether the change in the room improves the whole. (This is a fundamental principle of system design.) If the change in the room does improve the whole, the change will be made in both the whole and the part; otherwise not. On the other hand, to enable the house to function better, an architect may introduce a change that makes the performance of a room worse. For example, the insertion of a dumbwaiter going to a family room below may significantly reduce the work space in the kitchen, thereby making it worse; but it may also reduce the need for going up and down stairs when entertaining guests.

SOCIETY AS A SOCIAL SYSTEM

Society is a social system, not a biological or mechanical system. This means that its parts as well as the system as a whole can make choices and therefore display purpose. The parts of either a mechanical system (for example, an automobile or a clock) or a biological system (such as a person) cannot make choices.

Furthermore, large social systems may contain smaller social systems that have purposes of their own, for example, nations that contain states, states that contain cities, and cities that contain communities.

> *A community is a social system whose members share and pursue at least one common objective and which provides its members with, or provides them access to, instruments and resources that facilitate their pursuit of some of their common objectives—for example, police and fire protection, water, and trash removal.*

For us, communities are the elements out of which a society is formed:

> *A society is a social system whose parts are communities that have a common culture, and by a culture we mean a common view of reality and the same habitual ways of carrying out the community's functions.*

When a system is viewed as a social system, it is seen as having an obligation to its parts (which have purposes of their own) and to the larger systems of which it is a part (which have purposes of their own). The overall obligation a society has to all it affects is to contribute to their development. Development is not the same as growth. For example, a cemetery grows but does not develop, but Einstein continued to develop long after he stopped growing. Growth is an increase in size or number. *Development is an increase in one's ability and desire to satisfy one's needs and legitimate desires and those of others.* A legitimate desire is one that does not reduce the ability and desires of others to satisfy their needs and desires.

Treatments for Problems

*Problems are choice situations in which what is done
makes a significant difference to those who make the
choice.*

Problems consist of either opportunities (which potentially increase or create value) or threats (which potentially reduce or destroy
value).

Problems can be treated in four different ways—absolution, resolution, solution, and dissolution—and these form a hierarchy, meaning
that each is less effective, in general, than the one that follows it.

Absolution means to ignore a problem and hope it will solve itself
or go away of its own accord.

Resolution means to employ behavior previously used in similar
situations, adapted if necessary, so as to obtain an outcome that is good
enough. This approach to problems relies heavily on past experience,
trial and error, qualitative judgment, and so-called common sense. It is
the approach to problems most commonly used by those who govern and
those who manage public processes. Moreover, this approach has little
lasting power because it deals with symptoms and short-term effects, not
causes. Witness the continuing struggle between labor and management
despite more than a century of collective bargaining.

The third way to treat a problem, *solution*, means to discover or
create behavior that yields the best, or approximately the best, possible
outcome, one that "optimizes."

Problem solving usually involves research, often using experimen-
tation, quantitative analysis, and uncommon sense.

Unfortunately, few problems, once solved, stay that way; changes
in the environment, changing societal goals, and new information cause
solutions to deteriorate. For example, streetcars (trolleys) once solved urban transportation problems. They no longer do so; today they are considered to contribute to the congestion in an automobile-dominated environment. Furthermore, the first three ways of solving problems generally
do not change the structure or functions of the entity that uses them.

Moreover, solutions generally do not exist in isolation from other
problems. Solutions obtained to problems isolated from the other problems with which they interact generally produce one or more new prob-

lems. These are often more serious and difficult to solve than the original problem. For example, the use of insecticides to control crop-destroying insects created a number of health problems involving plants and animals (including humans) that are more serious than the problems they solved.

Dissolution, the fourth way to treat a problem, means to redesign either the society that has the problem or its environment in such a way as to eliminate the problem or the conditions that caused it, thus enabling the society involved to do better in the future than the best it can do today.

The differences between the four types of treatment are illustrated by the following example:

A major city in Europe uses double-decker buses for public transportation. Each bus has a driver and a conductor. The driver is seated in a compartment separated from the passengers by a glass panel. The closer the driver keeps to the schedule, the more the driver is paid. The conductor collects (variable) zoned fares from passengers, issues receipts, collects them from disembarking passengers, and checks them to see that the correct fare has been paid. Passengers can signal the driver (by pulling a cord) when they want to get off at the next stop. The conductor is supposed to signal the driver to move on when the bus has finished discharging and loading passengers.

Undercover inspectors rode the buses periodically to determine whether conductors collected all the fares and issued and checked receipts. Failure to collect a fare was taken to be much more serious than failing to collect a receipt. The fewer errors the inspectors observed, the more the conductors were paid.

To avoid delays during rush hours, conductors usually let passengers board the buses without collecting their fares, which they subsequently tried to collect between stops. Because of crowded conditions on the buses during rush hours, conductors could not always return to the entrance to signal the driver when to move on after a stop. This required the driver to determine when to do so by using a rearview mirror. Since conductors were not evaluated on how frequently they signaled the driver to restart after a stop, they sacrificed this function for collection of fares. As a result, drivers were frequently needlessly delayed. This led to a number of violent confrontations between drivers and conductors. The hostility and violence were exacerbated by the fact that the drivers and conductors had different and hostile unions, and the conductors were generally immigrants and members of a minority race discriminated against by native drivers.

At first, management did nothing (*absolution*), hoping that the drivers and conductors would solve the problem themselves. They didn't, and the problem got worse. Increased public pressure forced management to consider doing something. It tried to *resolve* the problem by going back to a previous, more desirable state by discontinuing the incentive payments to drivers and conductors. Both unions rejected this proposal because it would reduce their members' income. They also rejected a subsequently proposed *solution* developed by consultants: that the drivers and conductors share equally their combined incentive payments. Both drivers and conductors refused to increase their dependence on the other, even though it might increase their income. They did not trust each other.

The problem was then handed over to a consultant on organizational effectiveness. Several efforts to resolve the problem by bringing sides together for discussions failed. The consultant then turned to a friend, a systems thinker, for help. The friend wanted to know how many buses operate in the system at peak hours—that is, the size of the containing system. In spite of believing this number to be irrelevant, the consultant dug out the answer: 1,250 buses operated at peak hours. The friend then asked, "How many stops are there in the system?" This question also seemed irrelevant, but once again, under pressure, the consultant reluctantly returned to the files and obtained a map of the system. Together they counted the stops; there were about 850 of them. During rush hours there were more buses operating than there were stops in the system. (Stops were about three blocks apart.)

The consultant's friend then suggested that conductors be taken off the buses at peak hours and placed at the stops. There they could collect fares from people who were waiting for buses, could check the receipts of all those disembarking, and could always be in a position to signal the drivers when to move on. (This is exactly what is done on British trains, and in the Washington, D.C., metro system, ticket-issuing and -collecting machines are similarly distributed.)

The number of conductors required at peak hours was thereby significantly reduced. At off-peak hours, conductors were moved back onto the buses. This enabled most conductors to work an eight-hour shift rather than the four-on, four-off, four-on necessitated by peak usage. The displaced conductors were assigned to other productive work.

As this case illustrates, the dissolution of a problem requires *redesign* of the system that has the problem, a subject to which we return below. Design may, and often does, incorporate research and even trial and error, but it is the most effective way of treating systemic problems.

Idealized Design

An idealized redesign of a system is a design of that system its designers would have right now if they could have any system they wanted, subject to three requirements:

1. The design must be technologically feasible.
2. It must be operationally viable.
3. It must be capable of rapid and effective learning and adaptation, of improving itself, and of being improved from without.

First, an idealized design must be technologically feasible. New uses of available technology are not precluded, but the design must not be a work of science fiction. For example, mental telepathy cannot be used as a way for governmental units to communicate with one another and their constituencies, but a dedicated communication satellite or optical fiber network, neither of which may currently exist, can be used.

Second, the design must be operationally viable, capable of surviving in the current environment if it comes into existence. It must conform to current laws and regulations, be subject to audits, and so on. This ensures the conceptual feasibility of the design, not its implementability. Implementability is not required of an idealized design, only an approximation of it. Realization of this approximation becomes the objective of planning.

Third, the entity designed must be capable of rapid and effective learning and adaptation, of improving itself, and of being improved from without. Without learning and adaptation, a society cannot develop and improve. Because an ideally designed system should be capable of improving itself or being improved, it is *not* an ideal or utopian system, but the best *ideal-seeking* system its designers can conceive of at the present time.

Once the design is completed, planning is directed at closing the gaps between the existing system and its idealized redesign. There is no more effective way for a system's members to create a desirable future of a system than by continuously approaching its idealized redesign. A principal, if not the principal, benefit derived from such design-based planning is the learning obtained from engaging in the process. The process enables its participants to discover how much they know about the system involved that they have not previously been able to use. They also learn how much they do not know that they need to know in order to improve the system as much as possible.

In idealized design and the planning that incorporates it, process may well be the most important product, because it generates understanding of the system designed and commitment to implementing the plans coming out of it. This commitment stems from the principle that people own what they create. People willingly are more involved and enthusiastic about implementing a design when they play a role in its creation than when one is imposed upon them.

Idealized redesign of a system begins with the assumption that the system involved—for example, a nation, a family of nations, or a community—no longer exists, but its environment is assumed to remain untouched. If the redesigned system is a part of a larger system, and most are, the larger (containing) system is initially (not subsequently) assumed to remain as it was; only the system involved is assumed not to exist. The reason for hypothetically destroying the system is to enable the designers to think about it without the constraints that inhibit creativity. Starting from scratch stimulates creativity more than any other process.

Ideally, all the stakeholders in a system should participate in its idealized redesign. Since simultaneous involvement of all members of a society is not feasible, however, it is usually necessary to employ a sequential process. This involves initial design by a relatively small core group. The group's tentative designs are then widely circulated along with solicitation of suggested changes and additions. These should subsequently be taken into account by the core group, and the modified design that results should be recirculated. This cycle should be repeated until no new changes are suggested.

As we said in the preface, the designs that follow in this book came from using this process.

2   Governance

A government is the only known vessel that leaks from the top.

James Reston

Few would deny that the governance of our society and that of most others can be improved. A vision of how they could be improved might stimulate both the desire and the will to improve them. In this chapter we propose a design intended to provide such a vision, one that applies to virtually any society, whatever its size, and to the structure and functioning of its various components.

The principal values sought in our design are those associated with participative democracy. All democracies are participative to some extent, but not to the maximum extent possible. Furthermore, as government units become larger, individual participation decreases. In large democracies, elected representatives govern. In some, like the United States, considerably less than a majority of eligible voters elect their representatives. There are 120 million nonvoting eligible voters. This yields a great deal less than the "public mandate" claimed by those elected. In addition, the public's direct participation in decision making through referenda is decreasing because of the cost and time involved. But, with recent developments in communication technology, participation can be made much easier and less costly.

We believe the reduction of direct participation in governance is due less to increases in size than to the hierarchical way democracies are organized and operated. We will show that when governments are designed and operated from the bottom up, "lowerarchically," a great deal more direct participation is possible even in very large democracies.

The Deficiencies of Democracy as Practiced

Democracy, as practiced in most Western countries, suffers from three common types of deficiency in government:

1. The decision-making (governing) bodies are not sufficiently representative, and opportunities for direct and meaningful participation in their decision making by average citizens are minimal. Minorities and the disadvantaged are almost always underrepresented. Even those who are represented have little opportunity to participate directly in important decisions or even to influence them. Lobbyists representing affluent organizations and groups with special interests have far greater influence than do average citizens, let alone the disadvantaged.

2. Most democracies either do not address or do not deal effectively with many of the critical issues facing the governed. Among the many critical issues in the United States are the lack of universal health care (Chapter 4), the degradation of public education (Chapter 5), the lingering abuse and ineffectiveness of welfare (Chapter 6), the growing underclass and its unemployables, the addictive-drug problem, the increasing maldistribution of wealth, and the amount of violent crime (Chapter 7).

Because the most important issues facing the government of a democracy are usually ones on which opinion is most divided, taking a position on them is risky for elected representatives whose principal objective is to be reelected. Survival in politics increasingly depends on the ability of politicians to evade questions put to them directly. Most politicians elevate the arts of evasion and ambiguity to new heights. They consider the electoral consequences of a vote on an issue before considering the merits of the available choices.

3. The quality of the candidates running for office is generally so poor as to deny the electorate the possibility of obtaining effective representation. Despite our system of primary elections, the

candidates in these elections almost exclusively come from party ranks; others have little chance of being elected. Moreover, the amount of money spent on a campaign more often has more to do with who is elected than the ability and qualifications of the candidates.

Many good potential candidates are turned off from running for office by pervasive negative campaigning, the very high cost of campaigns, and the intrusion of the press into their private lives. Many of those who vote do so *against* candidates they do not want, not *for* ones they want. Unfortunately, not voting is *not* an effective protest against the quality of candidates running for office, because one of them, no matter how unsuited, must be elected. In most elections eligible voters currently have no effective way of rejecting the slate of candidates offered to them.

PARTICIPATION AND REPRESENTATION

When the United States became independent and formed its own government, it had a population of less than 3 million. Only a handful of cities had more than ten thousand residents. It was a very small nation consisting of very small communities.

As is the case now, the government of the United States was initially divided into three levels: local, state, and federal. (Note that the thirteen original states created the federal government; the federal government did not create them. Like our design presented later in the chapter, the country was conceived as a lowerarchy.) Because the basic unit of government was relatively small and compact, significant face-to-face participation in its decision making was feasible and often took place through town meetings.

Several cities and about half of our fifty states now have a population that exceeds that of the whole country in 1776. However, despite the tremendous growth of the U.S. population, the structure of its government has not changed significantly. The United States has not adapted much either to the growth and changed demographic characteristics of its population (for example, the average educational level attained by its citizens) or to the tremendous changes in its environment and available technology. Most people live in large political jurisdictions in which they cannot participate in a way they consider to be significant, and consequently they do not want to participate at all. One voice among millions is not believed to make a difference. Government no longer is believed to be by and for the people, but by and for those governing and the privileged and affluent few who can "buy" elections and elected officials. Continuous revelations of the abuse of power by elected representatives and the undue influence of those who "buy" them reinforce public cynicism. Trust in government and those who govern is very low.

MISREPRESENTATION

The United States and other democracies are divided into geographic units whose residents select representatives to serve in legislative bodies at each level of government. But many of these geographic units contain people with diverse interests and opinions on major public issues. Because only a small percentage of a unit's occupants may share a special interest, special interest groups form across units. Although their members often do not form a majority in any geographically defined unit, they often have inordinate influence at a higher level, for example, the National Rifle Association and antiabortion groups. In this way special interest groups have significant effects on government.

Also, the proportion of disadvantaged and minority group representatives in legislative bodies decreases going up from local to national legislative bodies, because there are few geographically defined government units in which the disadvantaged constitute a majority. For example, African Americans, Latinos, and Asians are underrepresented at state and national levels. As the size of electoral units increases, the percentage of any minority they contain tends to decrease.

Segregation of, and discrimination against, racial, religious, and national minorities is at least partially responsible for their geographic concentration. Furthermore, electoral districts are usually designed by representatives of the majority to minimize the number of political units in which national minorities form majorities.

Discriminated-against minorities obtain representation only where they have been segregated and packed into relatively large slums and ghettos. The cost associated with acquiring such minimal low-level representation—a poor quality of life—is much too high. Segregation breeds discrimination, and discrimination breeds malrepresentation, which facilitates a "tyranny of the majority." Our design of a government precludes such a tyranny, and our design of cities (Chapter 3) makes involuntary segregation of minorities unlikely, if not impossible.

The design of government and the electoral system we offer is intended to increase participation in contemporary democracies. Our design also enables the public to determine which issues should be discussed by decision-making bodies, and it ensures at least one candidate for each office who is considered to be good enough by a plurality of eligible voters. Before we turn to the design of the government that does all this, we need to define the word *democracy*.

Democracy Defined

Webster's New World Dictionary defines *democracy* as "government in which people hold the ruling power either directly or through elected representatives." This definition raises at least as many questions as it answers. Elected by whom? How often? Who are "the people"? Who decides who they are? When and how does a person become a member of "the people"? Answers to these questions are important, because without the answers we cannot design a more democratic system of governance.

We believe a democracy should have three essential properties:

1. A society is democratic to the extent that all its members who are capable of understanding the consequences of the choices to be made can participate directly or indirectly (through elected representatives) in making these choices.

By restricting participation to those who are capable of grasping the significance of their choices, children, those not yet born, the mentally ill, and those deficient in other relevant ways are precluded from either direct or indirect participation in government. Nevertheless, their interests should be taken into account at least as much as the interests of those who can participate. Society must be responsible for the welfare of those who cannot be responsible for themselves and who have no one to act for them, for example, parents or guardians acting on behalf of children. The decision as to when one is able to understand the implications of participation should be determined by test, not by age. We do not permit people to drive without passing a test, and we should do the same with regard to voting. The courts should be responsible for seeing to it that those who do not or cannot participate directly or indirectly are adequately represented.

2. In a democratic society those individuals who can exercise authority over others individually should be subject to the collective authority of these others. This means that ultimate authority lies with the members of society taken collectively. Those governed should be able to revoke the authority they have given directly or indirectly to anyone. This raises questions about the percentage of the eligible or voting electorate needed to participate in the selection of representatives in order for their choice to be considered legitimate. This too is an issue our design addresses.

3. In a democracy all are permitted to do anything they want to do provided it does not reduce the opportunity or ability of others to do anything they want to do. Any activity that keeps others from doing what they want to do—provided that what they want to do does not prevent others from doing what they want to do— is prohibited. This prohibition ensures those human rights normally associated with democracy, such as freedom of speech and religion. It protects pluralism but precludes aggression by some members of society on others for any reason. One is not enabled here to harm others unless doing so is the only way to prevent them from harming others.

Design Requirements

In a participative democracy, authority and resources should flow from the bottom up, not from the top down. In other words, the government should be a lowerarchy rather than a hierarchy. The governed should be self-governing to the extent that they want to be as long as they do not deny others a similar freedom. Governments should have only as much authority as electorates give them, and the electorate should have direct control over its government. No level of government should have the right to appropriate authority or resources unto itself. The electorate should be the ultimate source of both the authority and the resources available to those who govern at every level, and it should establish the policies that determine how the authority and resources should be allocated.

Authority is normally considered to be "the power or right to give commands, enforce obedience, take action, or make final decisions" (*Webster's New World Dictionary*). This is *power-over*. But there is another kind of power, *power-to*. Power-to is the ability to get things done by exercising influence, not authority. These two types of power become more negatively correlated the higher the average educational and skill levels of those governed. Putting it another way, the less educated and skillful the members of a social system, the more power-over must be used to get things done; but the more educated they are, the less effective power-over is.

Consider universities, whose faculties are among the most highly educated workforces in the world. A university cannot be governed autocratically by those who try to control by command. Organization of teaching must be done by the faculty; no administration can know enough to control the content of most courses. Although a faculty cannot be controlled, it can be *influenced* by ideas and persuasion by leaders. In a democracy, the same should be true of the electorate; it is not controlled but is subject to the influence of its leaders.

The Design

Our design of a participative democracy is divided into five parts: (1) the structure of government; (2) the system of elections; (3) the operations and functions of governmental units and how they should make decisions; (4) how to debureaucratize and demonopolize government; and (5) taxation.

THE STRUCTURE OF GOVERNMENT

The basic unit of government should be small enough to provide an opportunity for meaningful participation to *all* its qualified members. Such units should be small enough to be governed by committees-of-the-whole, as in town meetings. This committee should reach decisions by consensus, not by majority or plurality rule. (Consensus-generating procedures are discussed in the Appendix.) The basic level (level-1) political unit would contain no more than about one hundred qualified voters, for example, a very small village or a residential block in a city.

Each basic unit would elect a leader from among its members. The leaders of about ten geographically contiguous basic units would form the next higher (level-2) unit of government. Level-2 units would be accountable for and responsible to their constituent (level-1) basic units. Leaders of the level-2 units would in turn form level-3 units. At each level the units would consist of the leaders of the units from which it was formed. This process would continue until the unit with the largest constituency—the unit most removed from basic units, for example, a nation—is formed. This most-removed unit would represent the society as a whole, but the basic units would be the ultimate source of its power and resources.

Members of the basic units would select the heads of units at each higher level. Every level of government would consist of leaders of the next-lower level of government. The leaders of every unit, regardless of level, would be elected (in a way described below) by the qualified members of all the basic units from which the relevant unit would be derived. This means that all eligible voters could be involved directly or indirectly in electing the leaders of all the units of which they are members, from the least- to the most-removed unit. At least two candidates for each unit would be selected from among the unit's eligible voters. Those nominated would not have to be a member of the unit for the leadership of which they are nominated. Nominations could be made by members of the unit involved or other groups, permanent or ad hoc.

Other officials—appointed heads of functional units (departments)—required at each level of government would be selected by members of the appropriate unit. This means that elections would be confined to the selection of heads of units; therefore, the number of positions involved in elections would be considerably fewer than is currently the case.

The leaders of units at every level except the highest and lowest would also be expected to participate in meetings in the next-higher and next-lower level units. Therefore, leaders of all units, except those at the top and the bottom, would participate directly in units at three different levels: their own, their constituent units, and the next-higher unit of which their units are a part. In effect, all unit leaders, except the top two and bottom two, would interact directly with leaders of *five* different levels of government: two above their own level, two below, and those at their own level. (A diagram of these interactions is shown in Figure 2.1.) Such interactions would facilitate the coordination and integration of all planning and policy making.

If the basic units contain about one hundred qualified members, and level-2 units are formed by bringing together about ten basic units, and so on, the number of people represented at each level would be approximately as follows:

Unit Level	Adult Population Represented
1 (Basic)	100
2	1,000
3	10,000
4	100,000
5	1,000,000
6	10,000,000
7	100,000,000
8	1,000,000,000

These numbers are not absolute. Several considerations would affect the actual number and size of units, for example, the density and dispersion of the population. In some places, a hundred people might be spread over hundreds of square miles. On the other hand, a city block with one office building may house thousands of people. In this case, floors or smaller areas could be designated as basic units. A basic unit contains approximately the same number of people regardless of its location.

Those who work in an area where there are no residences—for example, a block of stores or office buildings—should be members of the basic unit governing that area. People with more than one home would be able to participate in the governance of each basic unit in which they have a residence or place of work.

Legitimization of voting in more than one basic unit makes it necessary to design out the possibility of an individual voting more than once for the same office. This can be done as follows: People who are members of more than one basic unit can vote for any office to which they are entitled as members of these basic units, but no more than once

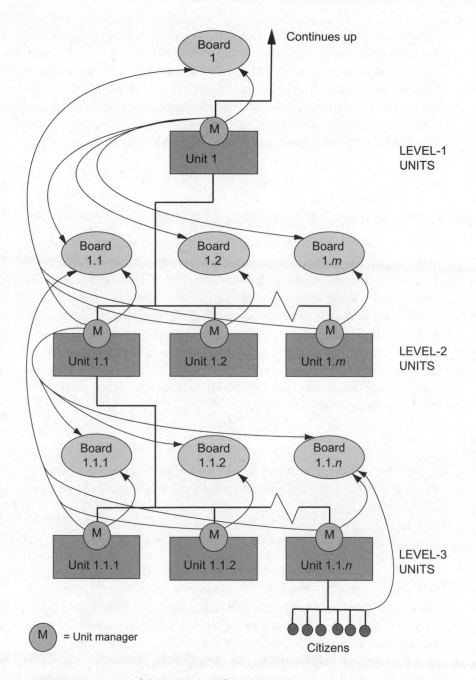

FIGURE 2.1   A Part of the Structure of Government

for any office. For example, in the United States as currently organized, a person with homes in two states could vote for all state offices but only once for all national offices. With currently available electronic communication, policing such a system would not be too difficult.

Most people have different roles at home, work, and play. These roles are normally carried out in different communities. Why, then, should participation in governance be limited arbitrarily to a place of residence?

Secession

Any unit at any level should be able to secede from the union of which it is a member with the approval of three-quarters of its voting membership. This may involve costs to the larger unit from which it separates. For example, the larger union from which the smaller unit seceded might have to establish custom and immigration stations on the border of the seceded unit. The seceding unit should pay these costs, the amount and method of payment to be settled by negotiation, arbitration, or a world court. The costs of maintaining these services would be covered by the unit from which the emigration took place. (This feature would eliminate most of the current civil wars and those that have taken place in the last half-century.)

Joining

One unit may join a higher level unit in a configuration of units of which it is not a part if majorities in both the unit joining and the unit joined agree.

Immigration

Ideally, a society should include as citizens all who want to reside in it legally and obey the law. This implies open borders. Legal immigrants would be those (without a criminal record as defined by the country to which they want to emigrate) who have either a commitment from an employer that ensures the immigrants' ability to support themselves above the poverty level as defined by the receiving country or a commitment from a person or an organization in that country willing to support them for at least one year, and a suitable place in which to live. The only exceptions to these requirements would be persons seeking political asylum or those attempting to escape from unjust persecution.

Temporary residential and work permits would be issued to short-term employees, such as migrant farmworkers, visiting professors, and students. Cost-free publicly provided services would be restricted to legal immigrants and those with temporary permits. Immigrants who have not obtained citizenship within two years after entry would be returned to their country of origin. The test for citizenship should include one for literacy in the country's dominant language.

To ensure a nation's awareness and responsiveness to the significance of emigration, the native country from which a person emigrates should be required to provide emigrants with transportation to their selected destinations with the proviso that this cost be repaid within three years.

The freedom to emigrate may well be the most important human right because it can be an act of last resort. Relatively free flows of people between societies can provide valuable feedback to those societies on their performance. In addition, movement from less developed to more developed societies would produce a more equitable distribution of wealth and quality of life among nations.

THE SYSTEM OF ELECTIONS

We believe the failure of a majority of eligible voters to vote can be reversed by a procedure that would enhance the role voters play in the selection of platforms and candidates.

At the bottom of each ballot there would appear an entry: *Someone Else*. To vote for *Someone Else* is to register a protest against the set of candidates offered. If *Someone Else* received a plurality of the votes, new candidates would have to be selected and the election rerun at a cost incurred by either those who nominated the defeated candidates or the candidates themselves. An amount sufficient to cover this cost would be placed in escrow before the election on behalf of each candidate. These deposits would be returned to every candidate who received more votes than *Someone Else*. This would be likely to improve the quality of candidates seeking public office.

Despite these changes, a significant number of eligible voters might still be unwilling to vote. In some countries, failure to vote is treated as an offense against the state; it is subject to a large fine or substantial punishment. We prefer treating voting as an obligation, not a requirement, which if unfulfilled would require the nonvoter to provide a specified amount of time to social service. The principle should be this: If one does not fulfill an obligation to society through voting, it should be fulfilled in some other commensurate way.

Political parties would be permitted, even encouraged, but they would be required to publish their platforms. Platforms should be more than a group of platitudes. They should include a statement and justification of objectives and the means to be employed in pursuing them, and the amounts and types of resources required and their sources.

Formulated platforms would be required of candidates for office at all levels. They would have to identify the political party with which they were affiliated, if any, or, if independent, publish their own platforms or those of special interest groups to which they are attached. An elected official who failed to fulfill campaign promises, or failed to make a significant effort to fulfill them, would be subject to recall by the electorate.

All election campaigns would be confined to (say) two months and be publicly funded, each candidate at each level would receive the same amount of financial support and equal access to communication media. No private funding of elections would be permitted. Every candidate would have a location on the Internet to which questions could be sent. The candidates' answers would be recorded along with the questions so that they would be accessible on the Net.

Candidacy for an office could not be announced earlier than three months before the election. A nonpartisan campaign board would be established to ensure that campaigning would be constructive, not devoted to denigrating opponents. The board would give one warning for negative campaigning; repetition would disqualify the candidate.

All terms of office would be six years. One-third of the members of every legislative body would be elected every two years. No one could be reelected to the same office more than once, or hold it for more than twelve consecutive years. A person would not be permitted to run again for an office held for twelve consecutive years.

OPERATIONS AND FUNCTIONS OF GOVERNMENTAL UNITS

The basic (lowest level) units would be able to do whatever they wanted as long as what they did had no effect on other basic units. If other basic units could be affected, the approval of those affected would be required or, if those affected did not approve, approval would be required by the unit at the next level at which the disagreeing units were represented (Figure 2.1).

Higher-level units would not be permitted to act on issues unless authorized by their constituent units. *All power and resources would flow from the bottom up, not from the top down.* It is for this reason that we call this type of organization a lowerarchy.

Low-level units may, for example, decide to run their own schools but delegate responsibility for police and defense to higher-level units. Whenever a responsibility is delegated upward, the units delegating would have to either provide the resources required to carry out the delegated responsibility or authorize the serving unit to charge for it. For example, a unit authorized to provide water to members of its constituent units could be authorized to charge them for the water they use. Clearly, economies of scale as well as effectiveness would be involved in all decisions to delegate or not. Publicly provided services would tend to settle at the level at which they could be provided at the lowest cost. As many government-provided services as possible should be provided on a fee-for-service basis.

Units above the first (basic) level would have two potential sources of income: disbursements from lower-level units and direct charges for services they provide. All taxes or changes in taxes would have to be approved by a majority of the basic units affected. Taxes would be collected by the unit that imposed them. The highest-level unit would be permitted to retain only enough money to carry out the functions authorized by lower-level units. The remainder would be disbursed on a per capita basis to the lowest-level units.

Budgets of all units would require approval by their constituent units. Units would be able to pool their resources to provide or obtain jointly desired services or facilities, such as trash collection, road maintenance, defense (discussed at the end of this section) or police, and fire protection. If there were alternative private sources of a publicly provided service, the public unit that provided the service would be required to charge for it and users would be free to use other sources. This competition would ensure efficient provision of services and responsiveness to users.

Units at all levels would make plans, policies, laws, and regulations but would not implement them. Unit leaders, not members of the unit, would be responsible for implementation. But every unit would be responsible for monitoring and auditing the performance of its leader. In effect, each unit is a type of parliament (making policies and plans) and its leader is like a prime minister, responsible for execution of the plans and policies.

Each unit would be responsible for seeing to it that the plans, policies, laws, and regulations of its constituent units were coordinated so as to resolve any conflicts that arose between them. In addition, no unit would be permitted to make a plan or policy that is inconsistent with a plan, policy, law, or regulation made at a lower constituent level without its approval. However, conflict or disagreement between levels is unlikely to occur because each unit, except the bottom and top two, would contain unit members of both two higher-level units and two lower-level units; these members would reveal potential sources of conflict or inconsistency. Few plans or policies would be likely to be made that had unforeseen negative impact on more- or less-removed units.

Decisions by Consensus

Decisions made by the majority in a decision-making body often create a dissatisfied and poorly served minority. Tyrannies by majorities, as well as by minorities, are to be avoided. Decision making by consensus avoids such abuse, but it incorrectly appears to make reaching a decision very difficult if not impossible. This is not the case, because consensus does not require agreement on what is the best thing to do, only on what is better to do than doing nothing. The following example illustrates this point.

The managers of an organization were divided into eight groups, each of which was asked independently to prepare an idealized redesign of that organization. When all had completed this task, they assembled and presented their designs to the total group. The chief executive asked for an expression of opinion to determine which of the eight designs was preferred. He received about a one-eighth vote for each. None received even a majority vote. At a loss for what to do, he turned to the consultant who was responsible for the consensus requirement. The consultant suggested that if the executive asked the right question he would be likely to receive complete agreement. The CEO challenged the consultant to ask such a question. The consultant gave the assemblage the following choice: keep the current organization without change or allow the CEO to make a random choice of one of the eight designs presented. The vote was unanimous in favor of the CEO's random choice. He did not have to make it because once the teams recognized their agreement on what is better, not best, they went back to work and came up with a design that had unanimous approval. Agreement in practice is agreement to act in a specified way; it does not require that the approved action be thought by all to be the best possible.

In group-design processes, consensus on most design decisions is reached without any special effort. When consensus is not reached, an attempt should first be made to design a test of the alternatives proposed, a test that all the participants accept as fair and the outcome of which they are willing to accept and act on. Design of such a test is relatively easy when the disagreement can be transformed into a question of fact; most such disagreements can be.

For example, an indigenous community in a very remote part of Mexico could not agree on whether to permit capital punishment for capital crimes. Some argued that such punishment was necessary for deterring capital crimes; others argued that it had no such effect since capital crimes were committed in circumstances in which consideration of consequences was very rare. What appeared to be a disagreement over values turned out to be a disagreement over a question of fact: Does capital punishment deter capital crimes?

A retrospective experiment was designed in which there was no need to kill anyone. The village members unanimously agreed to the test and to abide by its outcome. The states in Mexico were divided into four categories:

1. Those that did not have capital punishment five years earlier and still did not have it
2. Those that had capital punishment five years earlier and still had it
3. Those that had it five years ago but discontinued it in the last five years
4. Those that did not have it five years ago but introduced it in the last five years.

By comparing the changes in the number of capital crimes in each category, it was possible to determine whether capital punishment had any deterrent effect. The test revealed that the number of capital crimes *in Mexico* was not reduced by capital punishment (Figure 2.2). The village made capital punishment illegal.

Many apparent differences of value can be reformulated as questions of definition or fact. For example, the current so-called abortion issue depends critically on when life begins. This is a question of fact that depends on the definition of "life." Unless a definition can be agreed upon by the opposing sides, there can be no resolution of the issue. If the public debate focused on a definition of life, agreement might ultimately be reached because neither side wants to kill living beings.

A structured, although somewhat lengthy, way of discussing differences frequently generates agreement. It is an extension of a debating procedure designed by Anatol Rapoport (1960) and is described in the Appendix.

When Consensus Cannot Be Reached

A group can reach consensus on how to handle a situation in which consensus as it is normally thought of cannot be reached. The group can, for example, agree unanimously that in such situations the group leader should make the decision, but only if the group cannot reach consensus after the leader has revealed what will be done if the group fails to reach agreement.

This, or whatever other procedure is used when consensus cannot otherwise be reached, should itself be accepted beforehand by consensus. We have never encountered a case in which the procedures described here have not been considered to be fair and have not been accepted unanimously. Moreover, in the many participative design sessions in which we have been involved, we have never experienced one in which consensus could not be reached by one of the procedures described here. With experience, consensus becomes progressively easier to attain. We have, however, experienced situations in which the conflicting parties refuse to meet, as occurred in the early 1990s in Northern Ireland.

Military

Earlier in this section we said that defense is a proper function of government. In our design, however, no society would be permitted to

POSSIBLE TRUE CONDITIONS

	Capital punishment deters capital crimes	Capital punishment does not deter capital crimes
POSITIONS TAKEN		
For capital punishment	(Correct)	Error 1
Against capital punishment	Error 2	(Correct)

FIGURE 2.2   Possible Errors on the Issue of Capital Punishment

have any type of military force. The only permissible military force would belong to a world government, but its individual members would be recruited from all its member societies. Enlistment, all voluntary, would require literacy in an agreed-upon world-language. The salaries this military force would have to pay to obtain the number and quality of volunteers it wants would reflect the public's evaluation of its services. This force would be used only to stop either armed aggression within or between units and to provide assistance and relief where there have been natural disasters.

DEBUREAUCRATIZING AND DEMONOPOLIZING GOVERNMENT

Subsidized service organizations (in or out of government) do not depend on those they serve for their income and hence tend to be unresponsive to the needs and desires of those they serve. These servers are generally more concerned with the desires of their subsidizers than those of their users. If, in addition, such an organization is the only permissible source of the goods or services it provides—as government departments usually are—it is a monopoly.

Monopolies cannot be evaluated by the responses of those they serve, since those served have no choice. Monopolies tend to be evaluated by their size; the larger they are, the more important they are assumed to be. Therefore, they seek growth often by making work, work with no useful output; that is, they bureaucratize. A bureaucracy is an organization whose principal purpose is to keep people busy producing nothing of use. Unfortunately, although "make-work" has no useful product, it often obstructs those who have productive work to do. "Red tape" is such an obstruction. In addition, bureaucracy creates employment, however useless it may be, and this helps stabilize the political structure of a society.

The combination of bureaucracy and monopoly usually results in the worst possible service. Today, unfortunately, most government service agencies are bureaucratic monopolies. If government service agencies are to be productive and user-oriented, they must be debureaucratized and demonopolized. We propose doing so in the following ways:

1. Whenever a publicly provided service can be provided by one or more private sources, the public source should be required to compete with private sources for the right to provide the service, and, if this right is awarded to only one, the award should have a relatively short duration after which bidding for the right is reinitiated. This will prevent any service source from becoming complacent and unresponsive to its users.

2. Potentially competitive service sources should be requested to submit proposals for the right to provide these services, and the proposals should be open and revealed to the public. This would prevent any hanky-panky in awarding contracts.

3. When possible, consumers should be required to pay directly for the services they receive, thus ensuring responsiveness to consumers as long as alternative sources of supply are available. This would make usage by consumers more rational than if their costs were hidden and would also eliminate the need for benchmarking.

4. When consumers are not able to pay for the services they need, the consumers should be subsidized, not the service providers. Again, as long as there are multiple sources of supply, making income dependent on consumer choice would keep the system responsive to its consumers. This is the principle used in the United States in issuing food stamps. In contrast, in Mexico, where the providers were at one time subsidized (by a government agency called CONASUPO), the prices the poor paid for basic food commodities were frequently higher than those paid by the more affluent, who bought them through normal competitive channels.

5. When a service must be provided by a government agency, create as many different public sources as possible and make each dependent on consumer choice for its survival. For example, in Mexico City a centralized licensing bureau was notorious for its poor service. As a result, the mayor was subjected to considerable criticism and pressure. He turned the problem over to members of his staff. They came up with the following solution: Licensing bureaus were opened up in storefronts all over the city. Those wanting a license could apply at any of them. However, the only income a service center received was a fee from the city for each license it issued. Any unit that failed to issue enough licenses to cover its costs of operation would be reduced in size or closed. This arrangement brought an end to monopoly and bureaucracy. The quality of the service provided improved dramatically, and corruption was virtually eliminated.

6. When one or more public sources of a service are available, they should be permitted to engage in price competition. Price fixing would not be permitted. For example, if multiple bridges cross a river connecting two cities, these bridges should not be required to charge the same tolls, and price fixing should not be permitted between them. This would intensify competition that serves the consumers' interests.

7. When a public-supplying agency must be subsidized, the subsidy should be based on the amount and quality of service rendered. For example, a subsidy of a state university should be directly proportional to the number and type of students who are enrolled in it, provided the students have a choice of universities. The number of students applying would be indicative of the university's quality. Similarly, professors' salaries should reflect the number of students voluntarily enrolled in their courses.

TAXATION

A low-saving, slow-growing economy such as the United States would benefit greatly from shifting the national revenue system from taxing *income* to taxing *consumption*. That change would provide a powerful incentive to increase the nation's saving and investment and, at the same

time, increase economic growth and living standards. (Weidenbaum 1992, p. 1)

Twenty years ago, Martin S. Feldstein, chairman of the Council of Economic Advisers in the Reagan administration, argued that economic growth in the United States could best be promoted by taxing only the portion of income that is devoted to consumption. Such a tax, he stated, would discourage people from spending, thus boosting savings and investment (*Business Week* 1983, p. 80).

It has been suggested for many years that governments should tax consumption rather than income. The reasons are clear. An income tax can discourage efforts to increase income or encourage efforts to hide it, and there is no societal advantage to either. On the other hand, a consumption tax would encourage increasing income, discourage needless consumption, and promote savings and investments. This would stimulate economic growth and development.

The principal objection to the use of consumption taxes has been the difficulties involved in collecting them, keeping them from being regressive, and preventing cheating. However, these objections can be overcome by the following seven-part design:

1. A social security number would be issued to every child at birth and to every immigrant or long-term visitor on entry to the country. A bank account at a bank of one's choosing would be opened at the time the number is issued. For the newborn, parents would make the choice. Every organization would have one account using its employer identification number in the same way. Each person's bank account number would contain the social security number and the bank's identification number. Each person or organization would be permitted only one bank account. Each account would have a coded access number available only to the person or organization whose account it is. Deposits could be made without use of the access number, but not withdrawals.

2. All of an individual's or organization's income from any source would be required to be deposited directly in the appropriate bank account by use of electronic funds transfer.

3. Payment for any but very small purchases of goods and

services would also be made by electronic funds transfer from the purchaser's account to the provider's. Purchases could involve an instantaneous withdrawal from the purchaser's bank account and deposit in the supplier's account. If the required amount was not in the bank, the sum needed would be placed in escrow until payment was made. But the transfer of funds could also be postponed for as long as the parties involved agree to. The amount involved in a delayed payment, if currently in the bank, would also be put into escrow in the "paying bank" until it is withdrawn for the designated payment, thereby guaranteeing payment at the designated time.

4. Payment for very small purchases—for example, newspapers, chewing gum—would be made by vouchers of different denominations issued by banks in the name of the depositor. They would be nonnegotiable; they could be used only for deposit. These vouchers would be much like current for-deposit-only checks. When issued by a bank, their value would be subtracted from the amount in the receiver's account to ensure payment when they were received by the issuing bank. The vouchers would be machine readable and canceled by the machine that reads them.

5. Because all expenditures would involve a withdrawal from the purchaser's bank account, the bank would be able to prepare a complete record of each account holder's expenditures. Information on the nature of each expenditure would be on the record of withdrawals, including tax-exempt expenditures such as charitable gifts and investments.

6. Banks, if authorized to do so by depositors, would be able to file the depositors' consumption tax returns.

7. The consumption tax would be graduated. There would be no tax applied to those with very low expenditures.

Because money left in the bank would not be taxed and because the tax rate on expenditures should be greater than current interest payments on deposits in the bank, payment of interest on deposits by the bank would not be necessary; but savings would be greatly encouraged, much more so than now. The income of a bank would come from charges for the services it provides.

Money left in a bank and money owed to the bank would be inflated or deflated at the same rate as an appropriate government index and adjusted as frequently as that index is. Those who borrow money from banks would not have to pay interest but would have to cover a charge for providing and servicing the loan. These charges could reflect the estimated risk associated with the loan.

All of a bank's income would come from service charges and its earnings on the investments of the capital it has available for that purpose. Individual or bank investments in wealth-producing enterprises would not be subject to a consumption tax.

These tax principles would also apply to corporations. Their consumption, not their profit, would be taxed. This would encourage their efficiency.

There is another major advantage to such a system:

> Ridding society of its cash could make most criminal activity disappear, from purse snatching to drug trafficking. Electronic-money systems promise to lead the way toward a cash-free, crime-free society. (Warwick 1992, p. 19)

Public Decision Support Systems

Every major public discussion about whether to do something or not (e.g., pass a law) should be recorded along with (1) a statement of what the expected effects of the law or regulation are, (2) by when they are expected, and (3) the assumptions on which these expectations are based. The courts or other appropriate agencies at the level of government involved should monitor both the effects of the decision and the assumptions on which it is based. The appropriate agency would notify the relevant legislative, executive, or administrative body and the public as soon as it was apparent that either an assumption on which a decision was based is false or the law or regulation is not working as expected. An adjustment would then be made. Such adaptive changes in legislation, regulation, and implementation would themselves be monitored and their failure detected. This would facilitate and accelerate learning by decision-making bodies.

All laws and regulations should also have a designated time at which they would no longer be operative unless renewed. The designated time for lapsing should correspond to the time by which the full effects of the legislation or regulation are expected.

Summary

Democratic governments have degenerated in several ways. Their principal deficiencies are (1) decreasing participation in decision making; (2) inadequate representation of constituencies in governing bodies; (3) insufficient attention to society's most crucial issues; (4) the poor quality of most candidates who run for office; (5) unresponsive government service agencies; and (6) taxation that encourages useless consumption, illegal financial transactions, and cheating.

Our design of a democratic society or social system is aimed at eliminating the causes of these deficiencies and is based on three principles: participation, ultimate authority in the collective hands of the governed, and freedom to act in any way that does not reduce the freedom of others to act similarly. We designed a lowerarchical government that operates from the bottom up rather than the top down, where the power and resources reside with the people who transmit both power and resources upward. At all levels of government, people are represented by persons who are committed to voter-approved platforms.

Decision making in government units would be by consensus. By consensus we mean agreement on how to act, not necessarily agreement in principle. Seemingly unattainable consensus can be attained by testing alternatives, finding the underlying factual differences to what initially is a disagreement about values, and devising a process that enables a choice between the leader's view and that of the other participants taken as a whole.

Most services currently provided by government would have alternative sources of supply, public, private, or both; the income of all servers would depend on the amount and type of service they provide and the number of customers they attract. Competition among service suppliers would keep them responsive to the needs and desires of those served. These conditions would eliminate public and private bureaucratic and monopolistic servers.

Government would receive its revenue on the basis of personal and corporate consumption rather than income taxes. Under these conditions, government would be much more responsive to the needs and desires of the governed and would be subject to incentives that induce it to pursue efficiency and effectiveness.

Finally, all laws and regulations would be monitored to determine whether they are doing what was expected of them. If not, they would be adjusted or eliminated. All laws or regulations would have a designated time at which they would lapse unless renewed by the appropriate decision-making body. No out-of-date laws would remain on the books, as they do now, by default.

3   The City, Housing, and Transport

> Those who live in a city praise it to those who don't and castigate it to those who do.
>
> *Russell L. Ackoff*

The City

An increasing percentage of the world's population lives in cities. The Industrial Revolution accelerated urbanization and provided a higher standard of living and longer life to some but by no means all. To the affluent, cities made available more comforts, conveniences, companionship, culture, goods, and services than did rural communities. But urbanization also brought with it a new and more abject type of poverty. Since the mid-twentieth century, the quality of life in most cities, including those in the United States, has been deteriorating even while the standard of living of the affluent has been increasing. The post–World War II migration to the suburbs and exurbs in search of a higher quality of life leaves many cities or parts of them decimated.

The migration from artificial urban environments to more natural environments has become increasingly difficult because raw nature has been forced to retreat from advancing urbanization, suburbanization, and exurbanization. City dwellers have decreasing access to nature in the raw and to outdoor places where they can enjoy complete privacy. Most have to resort to crowded and littered parks, botanical gardens, museums, zoos, or nature programs on television to get a glimmer of what unreconstructed nature is like.

Cities have become increasingly congested, crime-ridden, dirty, and polluted, and many of the employment opportunities they once offered have migrated with employers to suburbia and exurbia. More and more of most cities are being reduced to slums and ghettos, open dumps in which discarded people and facilities are left to biodegrade.

We are witnessing the emergence of what has been called the "doughnut city," one with a core occupied by a decreasing number of businesses, and cultural and recreational establishments surrounded by ghettos and slums. Many buildings in the core are unoccupied or abandoned. In some cases portions of a city's core have been reclaimed and converted to high-cost residential and shopping facilities, but surrounding ghettos and slums have remained relatively unchanged.

The first rings around a city's center are usually inhabited by the poor, disadvantaged, and segregated minorities living in substandard, even condemned, housing. Such places have become reservations used to contain the poor. Expressways serve as concrete moats that separate the city's core from the suburban ring and provide access to the city's center without exposure to the ghettos and slums. The area around the moats, particularly on the suburban side, is usually heavily policed to inhibit unauthorized movement of the disadvantaged out of the city. Shopping facilities and places of employment tend to move out of the inner ring into the suburbs, essentially out of easy reach of those living in that ring. What stores remain tend to overprice their goods and services in order to cover their high insurance costs or losses through theft. Public transportation in these areas degenerates and is often discontinued. Graffiti and crime, much of it drug-related, proliferates. Inner-city schools have become out-patient detention homes in which young people wait impatiently to become old enough to break out or leave legitimately.

As the affluent move out of cities to the suburbs, and business and industry do the same, the city is deprived of more and more of its income from taxes. City governments are increasingly impoverished and dependent on charity and welfare obtained from higher levels of government. A huge number of city dwellers depend on public assistance. They tend to be viewed by the affluent as indigent and permanently unemployable by choice, a condition to which a new concept is applied: the underclass. This concept is used to "explain" the disadvantaged and absolve the affluent from responsibility for them. Some even argue that membership in this class is an inherited characteristic.

Redesigning the City: Requirements

Two interrelated conditions appear to be major contributing factors in the severe decline in quality of life in American cities: discrimination and segregation. Although segregation is usually a consequence of discrimination, either may appear without the other. But where they appear together, there is bound to be an inequitable distribution of opportunity. This is the most harmful type of inequity.

There are many bases of discrimination in modern society—race, sex, national origin, religion, age, sexual orientation, economic, and so on—but the most debilitating is race. Discrimination against African Americans is the most pervasive, but Latin Americans and Asian Americans are not immune. In most existing cities, neighborhoods or sets of contiguous neighborhoods are racially, ethnically, religiously, economically, or socially homogenous—the black ghetto, the Italian neighborhood, the WASP suburb are stereotypical examples. The variance between neighborhoods is greater than the variance within them. Urban segregation and discrimination further depress their victims, both economically and socially, and condemn many of them to life in a ghetto. Ghettos are the cancers of American cities.

We propose instead a heterogeneous city with no involuntary segregation in it *as a basic requirement*. Just as heterogeneity is healthier biologically, so too is it healthier socially. We would prefer to eliminate discrimination, but because it is a state of mind, we see no way to get at it directly. However, we believe that the elimination of segregation would significantly reduce discrimination. This belief is based on observations of the effects of desegregation that was imposed on at least some of the military during and after World War II. This desegregation reduced discrimination dramatically. One of us lived for many years in a completely desegregated neighborhood. While living there, our children did not develop a concept of "us" and "them." When we later moved to a suburban area, the oldest boy, then about eight, came home one day from school and asked what a "nigger" was. As long as housing and residential areas are segregated, desegregation of such things as schools, theaters, restaurants, and transportation have little effect on discrimination. Discrimination is learned and segregation teaches it.

In the heterogeneous city, the composition of each part would be the same as that of the city and its surroundings as a whole. This would convert the city into a *fractal, one in which each part has the same demographic mix as the whole: each part would approximate a representative sample of the whole.* The within-group variance would be much greater than the between-group variance. Although homogeneity implies that the demographic composition of each part of the city is like that of every other part, it does not mean they must be alike in other respects, for example, architecturally and religiously.

We want also to eliminate segregation without depriving people who have common interests from living near one another. Voluntary proximity, by itself, is not segregation. The key lies in freedom of choice. But even voluntary groupings tend to give rise to what Ronald Laing (1967) called a "we-they" attitude that is the primary source of prejudice and discrimination. To avoid this attitude, it is necessary to guarantee that the right of like people to come together is not accompanied by their right to exclude others from their aggregations.

Those who are subject to discrimination are usually disadvantaged in other significant ways. What is even worse is that their children "inherit" their disadvantages. For example, it is very difficult for a child born in a black ghetto to escape poverty. It is almost equally difficult for a child born of affluent parents to "achieve" poverty. Accidents of birth—the socioeconomic characteristics of parents—have a significant effect on the eventual socioeconomic characteristics of children and also on their life expectancy.

We sought to design a city that would provide complete equality of opportunity to everyone within it—a society in which there is no correlation between any of the expectations for children and the characteristics of their parents. This is *not* equivalent to economic equality. What young people become depends not only on the opportunities they have but also on what they do with them. Thus we sought equality of opportunity not only in a general biological and psychosocial sense—for example, with respect to health, education, employment, and recreational facilities—but also in a specific physical sense, that everyone should have the opportunity to be near any type of public facility that is desired. To this end, we tried to design a city in which all occupants have equal access to all urban facilities and services and can live as close to them as they desire.

Another requirement imposed on our ideally redesigned city is to reduce the excessive amount of (often unpleasant) time spent in going from one place to another. We tried to design a city in which everyone would be able to reach any destination within the city or its periphery conveniently, comfortably, inexpensively, quickly, and safely, and to do so in privacy, if desired. To accomplish this, we sought a design that would make it possible for most within-city trips to be made by walking, and to provide effective and efficient mechanical aids to those who need but do not possess them. Our ideal city is predominantly a walking city, one in which most destinations are within a ten- to fifteen-minute walk. The next most-preferred mode of going from one place to another would be bicycling.

A primary intent of our design is to maximize pedestrian movement and minimize mechanically aided transportation. Where the need for mechanically aided transportation exists, our design focuses on mass transit in an effort to minimize the need for private cars. In addition, private cars are redesigned so as to substantially reduce urban congestion and pollution.

To enhance the quality of life of city dwellers, each residence should also be within walking distance of natural open space, parks, or countryside, and preferably open space in which inhabitants can find privacy in a natural setting. We tried to make the ratio of "natural land" to "built-up land" relatively high and to provide each dwelling unit with its own private outdoor space as well as access to large public open spaces.

A final requirement of our design is that it protect the environment and conserve natural resources and energy. The preservation of open spaces is not enough to ensure a satisfactory balance between artificial and natural environments. Nature consists of a great deal more than open spaces. Recognizing this, we tried to design a community in which (1) pollution of air, water, and land is minimized, (2) natural resources are used as sparingly as possible, and (3) resources that can be renewed by acts of humans *are* renewed. It has been estimated that if the current rate of increase of energy use were to continue, the surface of the earth would be hotter than the sun in four hundred years. The message is clear: we cannot continue to consume energy as we have done in the past. Heeding this message, we have designed the city to use less energy.

The Design

Each part of our conceptual city has the same configuration as the whole. The city is organized into four tiers: blocks, neighborhoods, sections, and districts. The cities shown in Figure 3.4 have populations of about 640,000 and 1.2 million, but the model can be further extended for a larger city if desired. The neighborhood, in which we have included eight residential blocks, can be designed to contain a different number of blocks. The same is true of sections and districts.

The parts of the city would be functional as well as physical. They would form a *lowerarchy* (Chapter 2) in the sense that ultimate power and resources would lie in the smallest unit, the block. Whatever power and resources higher-level units had, they would receive from lower-level units. The public space in each block could serve as a place for daily conversation, relaxation, and supervised children's play. The neighborhoods, sections, and districts would each have a multipurpose center serving the educational, cultural, political, economic, and recreational needs and desires of those living within it. The larger the city unit, the more diversified would be the activities and facilities provided. They would be most diversified at the city level and least at the neighborhood level.

The number of blocks per neighborhood, neighborhoods per section, and so on, would depend on the topography of the city. There are many alternatives that meet the requirements we impose on the design, but we show only one here: the square city. It is important to bear in mind that the design we propose is schematic (topological rather than geometric); it is not to be taken literally. Our design is intended to be a theme around which adaptive variations should be made.

THE SQUARE CITY

A square block is the basic unit of the square city (Figure 3.1). It would cover approximately one-ninth of a mile (587 feet squared) and have a population between 150 and 250. We assume an average family unit of about 3.5 persons or about forty to seventy dwelling units per block.

Nine blocks in the form of a (3 x 3) square would constitute a neighborhood. This unit would cover one-third of a square mile and

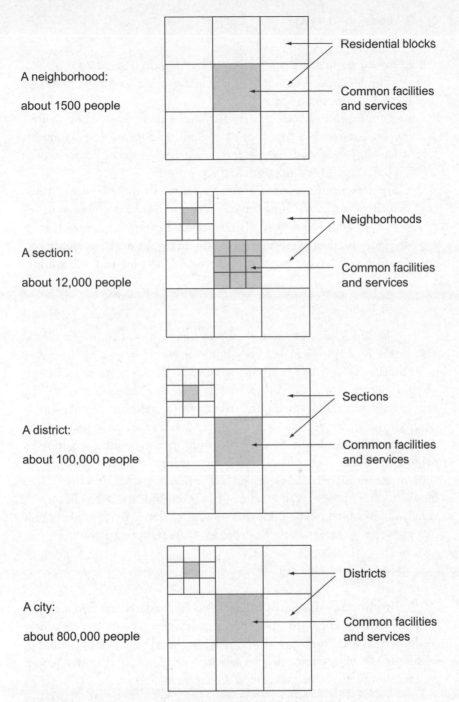

FIGURE 3.1 The Conceptual (Fractal) City

would have a population of between twelve hundred and two thousand people. The block in the middle of a neighborhood would be its center and its open or common space.

Eight neighborhoods clustered around a center would constitute a section. A section would cover one square mile and have a population between ten thousand and sixteen thousand. Each section center would contain open space for relaxation and recreation.

Eight sections clustered around a center would constitute a district, which would cover three square miles and have a population of between 80,000 and 130,000. Districts grouped around a center form a city. If eight districts were involved, the city would cover eighty-one square miles and have a population between 640,000 and 1.2 million.

THE BLOCK

The block is intended to be more than a physical unit; it would also be the basic political and social unit. It would have a participative government as described in Chapter 2 and be the ultimate source of all political power. A residential block could have any shape that suited the topography and the aesthetic preferences of the relevant population. It could consist of single, double, or multiple dwelling units. In general, the density of the population in a block would increase with proximity to neighborhood, section, district, and city centers. Figures 3.2 and 3.3 show some alternative block designs, all assuming an essentially square block. In each of these designs some private outdoor space has been provided, and in some, public open space has also been provided. Every unit of a high-rise building would be provided with an open balcony.

THE NEIGHBORHOOD

Neighborhoods consist of eight blocks clustered around a neighborhood center. They are designed as pedestrian islands whose center could be reached from any of the neighborhood's blocks by walking, without crossing a street. Each residential neighborhood center would contain shopping, the neighborhood government, and such social services as a nursery, day care center, and elementary school. This would make it possible for young children to go to school and for older citizens to get

1/9 mile

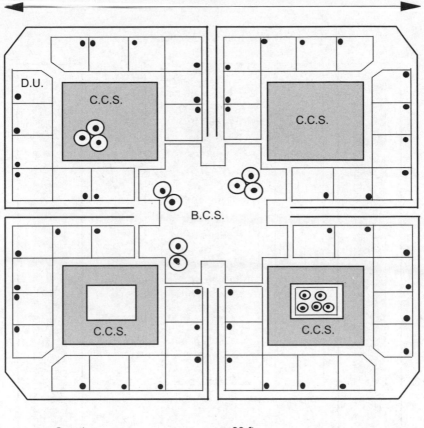

D.U.

C.C.S.

C.C.S.

B.C.S.

C.C.S.

C.C.S.

Courthouses:

60 ft.

60 ft.

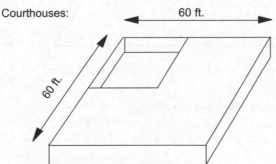

FIGURE 3.2   A Schematic Block Design
A block consists of 48–50 dwelling units, arranged in four clusters of 12–14
dwelling units (about 175 people) each.
D.U. = dwelling unit
C.C.S. = cluster common space
B.C.S. = block common space

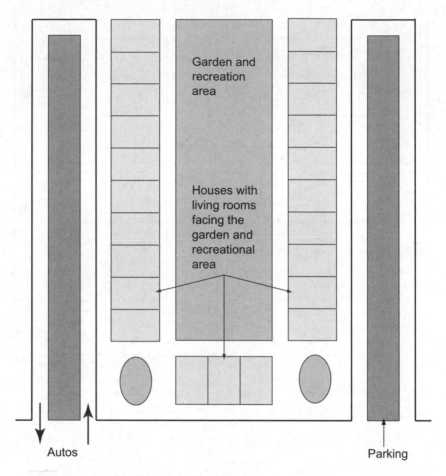

FIGURE 3.3   Another Schematic Block Design

their groceries without crossing any streets. The school should include an auditorium that could be used for neighborhood meetings, movies, plays, and so on. It would also contain indoor and outdoor recreational facilities to serve adults as well as children. In short, the school would be incorporated into the neighborhood's community center. Shopping would be provided by a number of stores of various types that could be supported by the neighborhood. These might include a convenience store, a drugstore, and so on.

Those who reside in a neighborhood would decide what activities and facilities its center should contain. After negotiating with contiguous neighborhoods in order to avoid unnecessary duplication, each neighborhood would decide what functions and facilities its center should have. The same principle would apply at section, district, and city levels.

THE SECTION

A section is composed of eight neighborhoods clustered around a center the size of a single neighborhood (nine blocks). The center would contain a middle school equipped with indoor and outdoor recreational facilities open to the public. It would also contain an auditorium for community use as well as such government and public services as fire protection, police, and health services. It would include shopping facilities and could contain high-rise dwelling units and professional offices. One or more blocks in the center could house small manufacturing units. The remaining blocks could be open space—maintained as close to a natural condition as possible—that could be used for recreation and relaxation.

Section centers and public transport would be within a ten- to fifteen-minute walk from all the blocks contained in the section and would account for most of the trips people have to make from their homes.

THE DISTRICT

The district is eight sections surrounding a center, which would contain a high school and junior college, a government and social services center, and recreational facilities, including a small stadium, shopping, industry, commercial and professional facilities, high-rise dwelling units, and open spaces. It would also contain health care facilities including a health care mall (see Chapter 4). Note that even the district center is no more than a thirty-minute walk from the most remote block it serves.

THE CITY

The city would consist of a set of districts, the number of which would determine the city's size. Layouts for cities of different sizes are

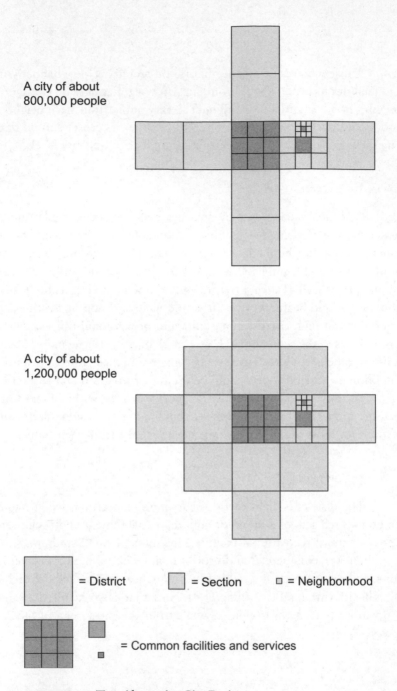

A city of about
800,000 people

A city of about
1,200,000 people

= District = Section □ = Neighborhood

= Common facilities and services

FIGURE 3.4 Two Alternative City Designs

shown in Figure 3.4. All land would be publicly owned and leased to oc-cupants for the duration of their occupancy. At the neighborhood level, all land on which a neighborhood lies would belong to the neighbor-hood. Section, district, and city centers would belong to the unit (section, district, or city) of which they are the center.

The city, district, or section would be able to gain use of a partic-ular piece of land by buying the structures on it for fair market value, but only if the occupants and the affected neighborhoods agree. Ultimate control of land and land use would be located at the lowest level of gov-ernment.

Housing

Inadequate housing and the destruction of our physical environ-ment are not necessary consequences of growth and development; some countries have avoided such problems—for example, Denmark, Sweden, Norway, and Holland. How can a society be designed so as to provide adequate yet inexpensive housing and facilities for all, and a protected and well-maintained physical environment outside the home?

PREVENTING THE DETERIORATION OF HOUSING

The deterioration of housing can be retarded, if not prevented, by taxing *the decrease in its value*, its depreciation rather than its apprecia-tion. Current taxes, based on the value of a house, encourage the genera-tion of slums and, eventually, abandoned homes. As the value of houses goes down, taxes decrease and it becomes easier to rezone them for mul-tiple household use. The income that can be derived from deteriorating housing is a consequence of current property taxing procedures.

The tax on a house or dwelling unit should be based on its market value, either an additional tax on the depreciation since the last assess-ment or a reduction for the appreciation of the property from its last as-sessment. This reduction should be equal to the amount of tax that would have been levied had the property depreciated by the same amount. Therefore, increases in the value of a house because of what an owner has done to it would result in a reduction of taxes, not an increase in them. This would encourage remodeling and proper maintenance.

The taxes on depreciation of property would be levied by neighborhoods unless they chose to transfer this responsibility to section governments. These tax receipts would be used by the taxing authority to maintain depreciating properties. The tax deduction for housing improvements and the tax on depreciation of property would virtually ensure good maintenance of property.

Much of the housing that has been or is being condemned would be rehabilitated. Able-bodied men and women otherwise unemployed would be trained to participate in such rehabilitation. To the extent possible, those so employed would work in the neighborhoods in which they live. Standards, materials, and supervision would be supplied by city agencies. The rehabilitated properties could then be rented or sold by the city at a low cost. In addition, anyone who volunteers to rehabilitate a condemned house should be given that house at no cost but subsequently be required to pay taxes on it. Such "urban homesteading" has been tried in several cities but has never taken off because the cities involved have not provided the kind of support required, for example, cleanup of the neighborhoods, conversion of open spaces into recreational areas, and improvement in the provision of public services.

Another reason urban homesteading has failed is the poor quality of the public schools in the neighborhoods where the housing is available. Young families that would otherwise be attracted by the prospect of obtaining their own home are turned off by the prospect of sending their children to what are usually the worst schools in an urban area. Use of the educational voucher system described in Chapter 5 would go a long way toward addressing this issue because it would give parents the freedom to send their children to the schools of their choosing.

NEW HOUSING

There is a worldwide need for good housing that can be built inexpensively, provide children with a protected place in which to play, and give adults a safe place to relax and recreate together with their neighbors. This need is probably best met through the use of row, or town, houses because they are the least expensive to build, heat, and provide with utilities. In addition, they are more likely to produce neighborliness than are detached houses. Solar heating should be used wherever feasible. All wires and pipes going to houses and on the street should be placed underground in easily accessed trenches. This design is meant only to be suggestive, not definitive. These houses could be built out of prefabricated sections or modular units that could be manufactured on site, in production facilities located in trailers.

The houses are turned around facing a parklike open area available to all the houses in a block. All traffic, automobile and pedestrian, would be confined to three sides of each block, the fourth side being attached to the neighborhood center without an intervening street. Because the houses have their garage entrances on the street side, there is not enough room for cars to park in front of the houses. Therefore, parking would be provided by parking strips located between housing blocks. These strips would convert streets into boulevards that preclude head-on collisions. Furthermore, mobile equipment for removal of trash, street cleaning, and snow removal would be unencumbered by parked cars. These streets would also be clear for ambulances, fire trucks, and police cars.

The interior walls of housing should be designed so they can easily be removed or added, enabling occupants to modify the interior to suit their needs and tastes; for example, a family that wants the living and dining areas to be one could remove the wall between them.

THE RIGHT TO ACCEPTABLE HOUSING

Housing that meets minimally acceptable standards should be a basic right of everyone, regardless of race, color, creed, national origin, or sex. Individuals with low incomes would be encouraged to build their own houses by being offered construction material and technical help at affordable prices. Housing choices would be available at hardware "supermarkets," located at section and district centers. Every neighborhood would be responsible for providing some low-cost housing that meets minimally acceptable standards. Rental of these houses would be administered by neighborhood governments.

Neighborhoods would have the right to withdraw individuals' rights to public housing if housing maintenance policies are violated. Residents would be responsible for keeping their housing in good condition, whether they own or rent. If a house were rented from a private owner, that owner would be responsible for maintenance of the property.

Part of the right to acceptable housing is housing in an acceptable location. One way of promoting socially rational location of residencies is to tax employers for the distance their employees must travel to work. This would encourage employment of those who live nearby and encourage those seeking employment to reside near the place where they would like to work. Such a policy could significantly reduce the amount of travel in the city.

Transport

Our city is designed to make it possible for most trips to be made by walking. The pedestrian scale is maintained through the section level, meaning that no more than ten minutes would be required to reach the section center even from the farthest residence. This would minimize dependence on private mechanized transportation. At the same time, public transportation would be available within walking distance to everybody. A convenient and well-functioning public transport system would further reduce the need and desire for automotive transport.

EXPRESSWAYS AND STREETS

Major expressways would be multilane two-way roads separating districts. There would be a peripheral expressway to make it possible for travelers to avoid the city and for city dwellers to go from one end to the other quickly. The airport and an energy management park should be accessible by expressway. Secondary expressways would be used to circle section centers, separate sections from one another, and connect their centers.

Ordinary roads would be used to separate neighborhoods from one another and connect their centers. Every street (those that are not expressways) would have a one-way bicycle and two-way pedestrian path on both sides. The sides of major expressways within the city should be lined with either soundproof barriers or green spaces to keep traffic noise out of residential areas. Very low density roads would be used to separate blocks and to provide access to neighborhood centers. They would be dead-end roads. Heavy traffic would be kept out of residential areas.

PUBLIC TRANSPORTATION

Subway lines would join district centers and connect these to the city's center. They would also join these centers to green areas, an energy management park, an airport, and other forms of intercity transport. At off hours, subways would be used to carry packaged waste to disposal or recycling plants at the city's energy management park and to distribute materials and goods.

Buses would be used to connect sections and section centers to district centers. They would run along the roads around section centers. There would be bus stops at all four corners of each section center. Then even the farthest residence would be not more than a ten-minute walk from a bus stop.

PRIVATE VEHICLES

Congestion caused by the automobile is choking many cities, for example, Mexico City; Santiago, Chile; Caracas; Bangkok; London; New York; and Washington, D.C. In some instances travel is slower than it was in the last century with horse and carriage. To solve this growing problem, our city allows only *urmobiles*, a design of which is shown below, on city streets between 7:00 A.M. and 7:00 P.M. from Monday through Friday. Use of such vehicles would more than double the capacity of city streets. Larger vehicles would be permissible at other times. Community-owned urmobiles would be available as drive-it-yourself (coin- or credit-card-operated) taxis at section, district, and city centers. Freight-carrying trucks and vans would be required to make their pickups and deliveries between 7:00 P.M. and 7:00 A.M. on weekdays. Community-provided ambulance service would be available at all times.

Congestion can also be reduced by reducing the need for automobiles. We have tried to accomplish this by dispersing common destinations within the city and encouraging people to live near their workplaces. We encourage increasing the use of public transportation, and we have tried to improve this by making access and use easier. The automobile now in use takes more space than necessary. It requires fundamental redesign for efficient noncongesting urban use.

REDESIGN OF AUTOMOBILES

Although most automobiles are designed to carry four, five, or six people, in most cities the average load is less than two. The mass-produced automobile was originally conceived of as a family vehicle. The average family size at the time was five or more, and this was the rationale for the six-passenger automobile. The family size is now down to about three, giving rise to the increase in four-passenger vehicles. But during workdays most automobiles carry only one person and most of the remainder carry only two people. So we begin by designing a two-passenger automobile for urban use during hours of heavy traffic, say 7:00 A.M. to 7:00 P.M., Monday through Friday (see Figure 3.5).

Speed is another factor. Most automobiles are capable of speeds considerably greater than posted speed limits on open highways, let alone the speeds often traveled in cities where they are forced to stand still or crawl much of the time. The maximum density of people in vehicles traveling on a flat surface occurs at about forty miles per hour. Our vehicle is designed to cruise at this speed, but not to go much faster

How should the driver and passenger be seated? From a safety point of view, the answer is clear: back to back. This means that in most collisions passengers would be thrown against the back of their seats. The driver and passenger would also be protected by use of air bags and seat belts, which would minimize injury and death. The motor can then be located where it maximizes the stability of the vehicle, in the middle, between the two seats. The motor need not be any larger than that currently used in a motorcycle. Then a simple frame and shell can be placed around the seats and motor.

The driving axle with a wheel at each end would be located through the middle of the car and directly connected to the motor. In addition, there would be one wheel at each end of the car, and the wheels would be geared so as to turn in opposite directions. This would enable the car to turn in its own length, thereby significantly increasing its maneuverability over conventional cars. Like electrified cars at amusement parks, the urmobile would have shock-absorbing bumpers around the entire car. Bumpers on all cars and trucks would be required to be at the same height.

The car should be capable of being driven from either end (but

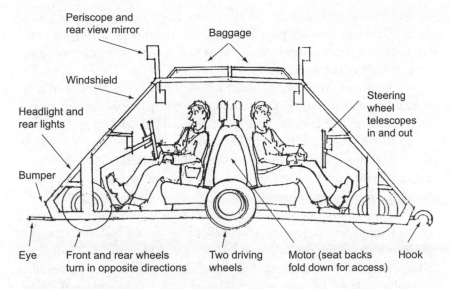

Periscope and rear view mirror

Baggage

Windshield

Headlight and rear lights

Steering wheel telescopes in and out

Bumper

Eye   Front and rear wheels turn in opposite directions   Two driving wheels   Motor (seat backs fold down for access)   Hook

FIGURE 3.5   A Schematic Design of an Urmobile
The doors slide forward on the left side of the driver and passenger—hence on opposite sides.

from only one end at a time). This would make it possible to park the car perpendicularly to the curb. (It would be shorter than most current cars are wide.) One would be able to pull into a parking space frontward without holding up traffic. In addition, since it could be driven from the other end, it could be moved out of its parking space with good visibility and without obstructing traffic. Controls not in use should be retractable.

Research has shown that truck drivers have fewer accidents than automobile drivers, in part because they can see over the cars in front of them and, accordingly, respond to more than what is happening immediately in front of them. For this reason, we have put periscopes on both ends of the urmobile so drivers can react to what is happening well ahead of them. Baggage-carrying space would be provided on the roof in a way not obstructive to use of the periscope.

In addition, from research we know that drivers who are anonymous tend to drive less carefully than those who can be identified. For this reason we believe that anyone who causes an accident should be required to carry an additional license plate identifying that person so that further irresponsible driving can be reported to the police. This is similar to the "learner's" license plate required on cars in some European countries. Their principal advantage is that they cause other drivers to approach such vehicles cautiously.

Each car would have a retractable hook at one end and a retractable eye at the other. This would enable any one of the cars to pull any other that was not able to operate. It would also be possible to have a cab just like the car but without a motor and controls. It could be hooked on to a car with a motor so that additional passengers (for example, children) could be transported. (In such an arrangement children would be seen but not heard.)

Preliminary estimates are that such a car would cost less than half of the least expensive vehicle now available; it would be able to travel at close to eighty miles per gallon of fuel and would be much less polluting. Also, electric and solar energy–powered cars would reduce pollution to virtually nothing. Because of its low cost, such a car would make automobile ownership available to large numbers of people in less-developed countries. And in many of them, neither air-conditioning nor heating would be required, further reducing the cost.

These cars also could be used as coin-operated do-it-yourself taxis. It would also be possible to have taxis with drivers, with or without a connected cab. Montpellier, France, and Amsterdam have experimented with coin-operated drive-it-yourself taxis. France intends to introduce a system called "Tulip," which combines concepts of private automobiles and public transportation. The tiny, urban-scale vehicles are publicly owned and maintained and are made available to subscribers at convenient local stations.

Renault, along with other French manufacturers, recently brought out a two-passenger urban vehicle that is a step in the right direction, although quite different from the one designed here. Ford has introduced a similar vehicle in Europe, the KA. Mercedes and BMW have announced their intention to introduce urban vehicles in the near future. General Motors has already introduced a small electric car for use in California, and Honda has a similar one ready.

TRANSPORTATION OF FREIGHT

Every city would have at least one *Trans Port* located at an easily accessible point on its peripheral highway. Trans Ports would provide facilities for intermodal transfers—minimally between air, rail, and trucks, and, where possible, ships, barges, and pipelines. They would provide (1) storage facilities for goods and transportation equipment, (2) repair and maintenance services, and (3) accommodations for equipment operators who are away from home.

Truck trailers would not be permitted to operate within cities between 7:00 A.M. and 7:00 P.M. Monday through Friday. This means that daytime deliveries brought to the city might require transfer to smaller vehicles at the Trans Port. Smaller trucks and vans designed for this purpose would carry standardized containers, thus minimizing transfer time at Trans Ports. All modes of transportation would use the same types and sizes of containers to facilitate transfers between them as is current practice for shipping and the railroads.

Unused rail beds would be converted into toll highways for exclusive use by trucks. On mixed-mode highways of three or more lanes each way, the right lane would be reserved for trucks and the left for automobiles. Dedicated truck lanes would have an electronic or magnetic guide imbedded in them so that automatic pilots in truck cabs could be used to operate vehicles. Some trucks would have double sets of wheels enabling them to run on rail as well as highways and to move directly from one medium to the other. Automatic pilots could be used here as well.

There would be communication-control points along highways or internal signaling devices on all vehicles so their locations could be determined at any time, as those of airplanes are now. Traffic control points would communicate information on road conditions and enable rerouting when necessary.

Truck drivers would be treated much like airline pilots are now. Their physical state and working conditions would be controlled and monitored to ensure their safety and that of others. There would be enforced limits on how long and how frequently they could drive. Driving while drunk or under the influence of drugs would be treated as very serious offenses.

Trailers would have couplings at both ends so they could be assembled into trains pulled by either a truck tractor or a locomotive. This would also make it easier to retrieve or remove crippled trailers. Trailer beds would be designed so that they could be stacked to ride on top of each other, permitting two or three empty beds to be hauled by one tractor. Containers would be loaded and unloaded by use of mechanized equipment.

All road vehicles would be equipped with radar control devices at both ends to prevent front- and rear-end collisions. The device at the front end would determine the distance to the vehicle in front and, using the speed of the vehicle on which it is installed, would determine when the distance from the vehicle in front is about to become unsafe. At this point it would take over control of the speed of the vehicle, signaling the driver to this effect. The driver would not be able to override this slow-down.

The device at the rear would make a similar calculation for the vehicle behind. When that vehicle came too close, lights mounted on the rear of the vehicle would flash at the vehicle behind it, signaling the driver to this effect. If the vehicle behind did not slow down, a sirenlike noise would be directed at it.

In addition to one-piece trucks and tractor-trailer combinations, there would also be trucks consisting of various combinations of easy-to-assemble modular units of five types: (1) power packs of various sizes to suit the weight of the load carried; (2) cabs with and without sleeping accommodations for one or two people; (3) chassis to receive power packs and cabs; (4) standardized weatherproof containers that lock into the chassis and each other; and (5) trailer beds of varying size and load-carrying capacity. Special-purpose trailers such as buses, concrete mixers, and dump trucks would be available, enabling more effective use of trucks.

Tractors and trailers would be available for a variety of new uses. For example, modular factories that could manufacture houses could be mounted on trailers. These could be joined on site to provide manufacturing facilities. Or they could be mounted on barges or rail cars and hauled from one appropriate site to another. Special-purpose classrooms (e.g., laboratories, computing facilities, and libraries) could be moved from school to school so that even remote schools could have the benefit of the best resources available. Hospitals could similarly use mobile equipment that is costly and not heavily used, for example, MRI devices. There could be assembly points at major entrances to limited access highways where automobiles could mount empty trailer beds returning home and be hauled to a designated destination for a fee. The automobile drivers could then sleep or work in their cars while being transported.

Summary

Our design of a city is intended to support a high quality of life. At the same time, it reduces many if not most of the physical and logistical problems associated with modern urban living, including undesirable neighborhoods, housing, and transportation. It reduces (if not eliminates) segregation—not by law, but by providing communities that foster heterogeneity because they are desirable places to live for everyone.

Our design gives people a real stake in being part of an urban community because of its governance (Chapter 2). It is user-friendly. We think it would reduce the flight to the suburbs by providing an alternative that could be more desirable than suburban living. It also would reduce the pollution associated with vehicular transportation, private and public, commercial and personal, because it maximizes pedestrian movement while minimizing fossil fuel–consuming transportation. The design promotes walking, bicycling, and mass transportation. It reduces congestion, thus increasing energy efficiency, and makes the transportation of freight more efficient.

Finally, our approach to the design of the city is one of high, if not maximum, flexibility. There are no "lock-ins." Our designs of neighborhoods, sections, and districts could be used for communities smaller than cities. The designs or parts of the designs of the housing and transportation systems could be adapted to any special need or circumstance of any size community and virtually any degree of population density. The use of systems thinking in the designs makes this degree of flexibility possible.

4   Health Care

More medical care does not equal better health.

   Aaron Wildavsky

The only way to keep your health is to eat what you don't want, drink
what you don't like, and do what you'd rather not.

   Mark Twain

   In the 1994 U.S. preelection frenzy to reform health care, all kinds
of proposals intended to improve it were offered, and they have continued ever since. But none of the proposals that came before Congress involved transforming (in contrast to reforming) the system taken as a
whole; they dealt primarily or exclusively with only one of its aspects,
usually financial. Nevertheless, it seems obvious that before deciding how
health care should be paid for, a system worth paying for should be created. In this case, the obvious is overlooked because it is widely believed
that the United States provides the best health care in the world. It may to
some, but not to all. Many—estimates go up to over 40 million—have no
health care insurance at all. The United States is now the only developed
country in the world without health care coverage for all of its residents.
   According to a survey of 191 countries conducted by the World
Health Organization (2000), the United States ranks 37 in quality of
health care, not first as its politicians claim. Yet it spends about four
thousand dollars per person per year on health care, and approximately
14 percent of gross domestic product, the highest percentage devoted to
health care of any country
   None of the proposals for so-called transformation of the health
care system offered would provide the incentives that would change the
behaviors of its two most important stakeholders: the recipients and providers of care. And just as crucial, they would not make the kinds of

change most needed to focus the system on the maintenance of health rather than on the treatment of sickness and disability. Furthermore, they would not significantly reduce the system's cost because they do not address excessive administrative costs, unnecessary testing and treatment, overprescribing, malpractice, and fraud. They would not change most of those aspects of the current system that encourage abuse. Meanwhile, more and more hospitals and practitioners are going out of business, and the number of those who are uninsured is increasing.

By itself, changing the way medical care is paid for will not reform the health care system. What is required is a comprehensive redesign of the system, not changes of any of its aspects considered separately.

The current system is not a health care system; it is a sickness- and disability-care system. Getting rid of illness, what we don't want, is not the same as maintaining wellness, what we do want.

The care providers, individual and institutional, in the current system are primarily compensated for taking care of sickness and disabilities. Therefore, their incentives, however unintended, are to preserve, if not create, sickness and disability, and provide unnecessary treatment and testing. For example, a headline in the *Philadelphia Inquirer* (September 12, 1999) read, "Health care's deadly secret: Accidents routinely happen." On the following day this newspaper reported that according to the "Harvard Medical Practice Study" published in 1991, "one out of every 200 of the patients admitted to a hospital ended up dead because of a hospital mistake." Many observers believe that there is too much unnecessary surgery, testing, and prescription of drugs. Observers have been writing about the "overmedicalization" of the United States for decades (*Daedalus* 1994).

There is a considerable difference between what is preached and what is practiced by health care providers; this difference is due not to the evil intentions of the servers, but to the incentives embedded in the current system. For this reason our design seeks to change these incentives significantly.

When completed, the design presented here was adapted and applied to the health care system operated by the Sisters of Charity of Nazareth Corporation. It covered seven hospitals, five in Kentucky and one each in Tennessee and Arkansas (Rovin et al. 1994). Aspects of the design were subsequently adapted and used in several other systems.

Beneficiaries of the System

Every legal resident of the United States not in prison, regardless of age or any other personal characteristic, would annually receive a health care voucher that entitles him or her to all essential health care products and services. Legal visitors to the United States would also be entitled to receive a voucher. Residents or visitors who choose not to use their voucher could use fee-for-service providers operating outside the national health care system, but they still would have to pay a health care tax.

Employers would pay a health care tax to cover worker's compensation, and they would be responsible for covering health care costs of unvouchered employees, such as illegal residents. This would discourage employment of illegal immigrants, hence their illegal entry into the United States, and would encourage those who are entitled to vouchers to get them.

Health Care Vouchers and Tax

Annual health care vouchers would be redeemable by primary care providers. Their redeemable value would reflect patients' health-related characteristics, which would be provided by the patients on their tax forms. This information would be endorsed by their primary care providers. The services and products covered by a voucher would not vary within a community, but the amount of these to which patients are entitled would vary depending on their health needs.

The tax applied to individuals would also vary. Tax rates would be based on individual profiles that reflect age, income, number of dependents, and other health-relevant characteristics that can be controlled (for example, smoker or not, recreational drug use or not, regular exercise or not, and such dangerous voluntary activities as race-car driving). However, the tax rate would not reflect the amount of unavoidable illness or disabilities necessitating use of the system. The poor might pay no tax but still be entitled to the same services and products as those who pay health care taxes.

Individual abuse of the system reported by the primary care provider would be reflected in the individual's tax rate but would not affect the value of that individual's voucher. A smoker, for example, would

have a higher tax rate than a nonsmoker. Counseling and educatio
programs would be available to which abusers and misusers of the system could be referred. Their failure to use health-producing services that
are prescribed by their primary care provider would be considered un-
derutilization of the system and, when reported, would increase their
tax rate.

Employers would not be required to pay an employee's individual
health care tax. However they would be able to reimburse employees for
all or part of their health care taxes as a benefit. If they decide not to
cover all of their employees' taxes, they would be required to increase
each employee's salary in the first year by the amount they spent in the
last year on that employee's health care insurance. This increase would be
permanent. No further health care–related adjustment in salaries would
be required. This provides another incentive to employees to engage in
healthy behavior and not to waste services to which they are entitled.

Health care vouchers would be distributed by the IRS, but it
would have no decision-making powers. All the criteria and information
it would use in issuing vouchers would come from another source, for example, the Department of Health and Human Services.

The Primary Care Provider

Each community's health care board (described below) would be
responsible for certifying all primary care providers. Primary care providers would serve as their patients' gatekeepers, advocates, and guides
through the health care system. Primary care providers would be one of
five types: internists, family practitioners, gynecologists, pediatricians,
and a new type of health care professional, a primary care nurse-practitioner, described below.

Because primary care providers would be responsible for paying
all reqired healthcare services authorized by the community health care
board, they would be inclined to use these services judiciously. They
could operate their own laboratories and other medical support facilities
without a conflict of interest since they would incur the costs of their use.

Primary care providers would be required to notify the IRS of the
death of a registered patient. The identification card of the deceased
would be submitted to a funeral director certified by the community
health care board, which would receive a fixed fee from the IRS on return

that card to the IRS. This would eliminate the fraud that currently occurs when medical bills are submitted to third-party payers for persons
who have died. Certified funeral directors would not have the option of
refusing to provide the specified services at the specified fee. However,
family or others related to the deceased could pay more to the funeral director for more than the minimal services, if they so desired.

A "renewal bonus" would be paid to the primary care provider
when a registrant renews registration for another year. This renewal
bonus would be an incentive to primary care providers to satisfy the individuals they serve and to provide the needed services.

SERVICES PROVIDED

The primary care provider would be responsible for providing any
services or products authorized by a local community health care board,
which will be described later. The services available would be the same
for everyone in a community, but the dollar value of their vouchers
would not be; the vouchers would reflect the expected service requirements as a function of individual characteristics. For example, the vouchers of the elderly would be worth more than those of young adults.

Essential health care would cover medical and wellness services
and products including those related to dental, optical, and auditory
needs. Services and products authorized would vary by community. For
example, frostbite could be serious up north but not sunburn, which is
serious down south. Elective services would be available to patients for a
fee, but they would not be provided by primary care providers operating
within the system. This would discourage primary care physicians operating within the system from prescribing unnecessary elective treatments,
which they might otherwise do in order to increase their incomes.

CHANGING A PRIMARY CARE PROVIDER

Individuals would be able to change primary care providers at any
time. One change per year within the community would be permitted
without penalty. Changes required by relocation of patients would not be
limited. Additional changes would involve a penalty. The person would
be required to notify the IRS of the change if it involved a change out of

a primary care organization. When a person shifts from one primary care provider to another who is not affiliated with the same organization, payments to the two providers involved would be prorated by the IRS depending on the date of change.

EDUCATION OF PRIMARY CARE PROVIDERS

Federal, state, or local governments would subsidize the education of health care practitioners who could otherwise not afford it. Those supported in this way would be required to serve for at least a specified number of years in the national health plan at a designated location. This would ensure the provision of required care in areas where providers would not normally locate voluntarily, for example, in sparsely settled rural areas or urban ghettos.

PROVIDERS OUTSIDE THE SYSTEM

Primary care providers would not have to participate in the publicly financed program. They could choose to practice outside the system. However, none would be able to practice within and outside the system at the same time. People using providers outside the system would have to pay the fees charged by those providers and for other health services they prescribe. Private insurance could be used to cover these costs. However, this would not excuse those who use providers outside the system from paying the health care tax referred to above.

MALPRACTICE INSURANCE

Malpractice insurance would be available to all health care providers from provider associations as well as private insurers. Arbitration panels (at least half of whose members are not health care providers) would be established regionally. These panels would be the initial point of entry of all malpractice suits. The panel would use screening procedures to determine which cases to hear. Cases that the panel refused to hear or panel decisions unacceptable to the plaintiff could be appealed through the legal system.

Appropriate tort reform in the fifty states should be enacted to reduce the exaggerated volume and costs to the system. This reform could incorporate all of the following: no-fault payments for injuries, limitations on noneconomic damages, shorter statutes of limitations, and elimination of the percentage contingency fee arrangement for plaintiffs' attorneys.

INCOME INSURANCE FOR PRIMARY CARE PROVIDERS

All certified primary care providers within the system would be able to purchase catastrophic (income-reduction) insurance that would ensure their earning no less than an amount that they would specify. The income-insurance premiums they would have to pay would be proportional to the minimum income they specify and their expected income. Such insurance would prevent primary care providers from being wiped out by adverse selection of patients, an epidemic, or a natural catastrophe.

PROBLEM PATIENTS

Unfortunately, some patients pose problems for their care providers. Problem patients would be ones who are difficult to deal with, not ones who are believed to require costly treatment. Patients who demand unnecessary treatment, consistently break appointments, and are demonstrably belligerent are examples of problem patients. Those problem patients who could not find a provider that would accept them would be assigned to one by the community health care board. They would be subject to higher health care tax rates. Their health vouchers would be worth more, but would not necessarily be more profitable on average, to the primary care provider who received them.

There would be an incentive for a primary care provider to transform a problem patient into a normal one: the provider would receive (an incentive) payment a year after a problem patient is authorized by the provider to register as a normal patient with either the same or a different primary care provider.

Patients who became ill because they did not follow the advice of their providers would have to cover the cost of any illness or disability that occurred subsequently as a result. For example, a person going on a safari to Africa who fails to follow the provider's advice to get an anti-malaria shot and who contracted malaria while in Africa would personally have to cover the cost of treatment of that disease. Treatment for such an illness or disability would have to be obtained from a provider not within the system.

Primary care providers who participated in the national program would be required to handle up to a specified percentage of problem patients as determined by their community health care boards, discussed in the next section.

A primary care provider who believed that a person was demanding unnecessary services could refuse to provide them. This would be entered into both the provider's and the patient's record. The decision could be appealed to a review board established by the group, institution, or integrated health care system, with final appeal to a reviewing body established by the community health care board. During the appeal process, patients could receive the disputed service from another provider. However, patients would be liable for the cost of services deemed to be unnecessary by the reviewing body. Those deemed to have been necessary would have to be paid for by the primary care provider.

The only other acceptable reason a primary care provider would have for discontinuing service to a person would be that person's refusal to follow instructions that the provider considered critical for the patient's health (e.g., to try to lose excess weight or to stop smoking or using drugs). Such information would go into the patient's record and increase that person's tax rate. These decisions would also be subject to appeal.

Community Health Care Boards

Communities would be the basic units for which health care systems would be designed. *Community* is defined operationally as follows: Select a small geographic area within which almost all the inhabitants use internally provided health care services. Then add a ring around that area so that most of the inhabitants of that ring continue to use services provided within the extended area. Continue this until most of the inhabitants in the last ring that has been added use services provided outside the circumscribed area. The enclosed area, excluding this last ring, constitutes a community. A "community," therefore, is neither a political nor a geographic unit, but a health care unit—one whose residents primarily use health care providers and services within it.

Community health care boards would be created to democratize the health care system and to ensure that the populations they represent receive the appropriate quality and quantity of health care services. Another purpose is to provide an oversight mechanism not subject to the whims of politicians and desires of special interest groups.

COMPOSITION AND DESIGN OF THE BOARDS

Essentially, the design of the community health care board would be lowerarchical, as described in Chapter 2 (also see Figure 2.1). For example, each block in urban areas and each corresponding rural area (both containing one hundred to two hundred people) would elect a health care representative who would serve for three years, a term that would be renewable only once. In high-rise living quarters, a representative would be elected by each one hundred to two hundred residents. A building of, say, six hundred residents would be considered to consist of three urban units.

The representatives from each of about eight to twelve urban and rural units would constitute a first-level health care board. Every such board would elect a chairperson who would also serve the next higher level board (for example, a neighborhood in an urban area). Higher-level boards would be similarly formed up to a community health care board. Chairpersons of any board above the first level would be replaced on all lower levels on which they served except one level down, where they would continue to serve.

Each board would include the director of each health care service unit that primarily serves the area covered by that board. This means that the directors of health care service units would serve on only one board, the one representing the largest area for which their unit can be said to be the primary source of service.

Summarizing to this point, each board would include a representative of each unit at the next lower level, from among whom it would select a chairperson who would then serve on the next higher level board. In the case of the community's board, the next higher level would be a regional board.

The chairpersons of any but the lowest and highest level board will participate in the next lower and higher level boards, and hence will interact with representatives two levels down (in the next lower level board), and two levels up (in the next higher level board) as well as with others at their level.

As with all other board members, members of community-level boards would receive no compensation. However, these boards would receive from the IRS an amount of money proportional to the population of the community. Communities would be able to tax their own members (with the members' consent, obtained by referendum) in order to obtain a larger budget for their boards.

FUNCTIONS OF THE COMMUNITY HEALTH CARE BOARD

The community health care board would function as follows:

1. The community health care board would certify all providers of health care, wellness and illness, for the healthy, sick, or disabled within the community. (Only certified providers would be able to cash in vouchers that serve as debit cards.)

2. The community health care board would create a community health care audit board, none of whose members come from within the community and of whose members no more than half are health care providers. Members of the community health care audit board would be compensated for their time. The intent is to have an audit group that would be above suspicion and have maximum credibility before the public, with professionals and in court, if necessary.

3. The community health care board would produce an ordered list of health care services, identifying those the health care vouchers would (and would not) cover within that community. The cutoff point on such a list could be raised or lowered depending on the health status of the community, the aggregate value of the vouchers, and the need. It could also be raised or lowered in order to increase or decrease the average earnings of primary care providers.

4. The community health care board would develop and maintain a community health care information system (Rovin et

al. 1994). This service could be contracted out, but if this were done, the community health care board would remain responsible for its effective performance.

5. The community health care board would establish a dispute adjudication board, to which all complaints, including alleged malpractice, would initially be submitted. The judgments of this board regarding malpractice would not be legally binding but could be accepted voluntarily by the parties involved. Appeal to the courts would still be possible, but the findings of this board would be presented as expert testimony in court.

6. Finally, the community health care board would develop and operate a community health care educational program.

THE FUNCTIONS OF BOARDS AT ALL LEVELS

Health care boards at all levels would function as follows:

1. Each health care board at every level would plan for the unit whose board it is.

Every board would be allowed to implement any decision that does not affect the domain of any other board at its own or a higher level. If one of its decisions would affect such a domain and the agreement of the responsible boards can be obtained, the decision can be implemented without further approval. If agreement cannot be reached, the issue involved should be taken for resolution to the lowest-level board at which the disagreeing boards converge.

Note that this arrangement eliminates the need to consider centralization versus decentralization issues because each decision reaches the appropriate level—the lowest one in which all those affected are represented.

2. Each health care board at every level would be responsible for policy making for the unit whose board it is and its subordinate units.

A policy is a rule, regulation, or law that governs decision making. For example, "only a certified surgeon can do surgery" would be a policy. Selection of a surgeon to do it would be a decision. In the United Kingdom, Parliament is a policy-making body that makes no decisions. Decisions are made by the Prime Minister. In this case, the chairperson makes decisions compatible with the policies made by the board.

Chairpersons may ask their boards for advice on decisions the chairperson must make, but however boards are involved in decision making, responsibility for decisions lies with the chairperson, not the board. Policies, on the other hand, are the responsibility of the boards, not the chairpersons.

3. Health care boards at all levels would coordinate the plans and policies of the next lower level (if there is one).

Each board is responsible for ensuring the compatibility of plans and policies made in all the boards represented on it. Since the chairpersons at the next lower level are on the board making these coordinating decisions, coordination is largely self-administered with the participation of two higher-level chairpersons. This makes the formation and preservation of organizational silos virtually impossible.

4. Each health care board at every level would integrate its own plans and policies and those of its lower levels with those made at higher levels.

5. Each health care board at every level would evaluate and improve the performance of the board's chairperson and its other members. Each would be responsible to remove a chairperson whose performance remains unsatisfactory when improvement is not obtained. Note that this set of conditions makes the system completely democratic and encourages cooperation between levels rather than adversarial relationships.

6. Health care boards at all levels would be responsible to bring to the attention of higher-level boards any health-related deficiencies or opportunities of which the higher-level boards might not be aware.

7. Health care boards at all levels would administer educational programs within their areas.

8. Health care boards at all levels would bring to the attention of the community health care board any individuals or groups

who they believe are not receiving adequate health care for any reason and would suggest corrective action.

9. Health care boards at all levels would maintain a continuous health care improvement program in their areas.

10. Health care boards at all levels would see to it that the physical and social environment in their areas is conducive to health. Where it isn't, they would take steps to correct the deficiencies.

Levels of Care

Care would be provided at as many as five different levels: primary, secondary, tertiary, quaternary, and extended care (see Figure 4.1). The actual number of levels within a community would depend on the size and density of its population. Primary care would be provided to urban neighborhoods and rural districts. Contiguous urban neighborhoods would constitute a section that would be provided with a secondary care unit. In turn, contiguous sections would be combined into districts served by a tertiary care unit. Quaternary units would serve large regions. Adaptation to local geography and demography would obviously be required. Where feasible, all or several levels of service would be provided at one location.

Primary care—including diagnostic tests, treatment, and wellness services—would be made available and accessible to individuals in their neighborhoods or rural areas either by a network of separate facilities or by an integrated health care center.

Extended-stay units would have facilities for the aged and those with an extended chronic illness or disability who require inpatient care or mental health treatment and custody. However, wherever and whenever possible, care would be provided within private homes.

PRIMARY CARE

Primary care would normally include (but not be limited to) the following functions: prevention, wellness, emergency, and outpatient services, including surgery, laboratory, pharmacy, home health, rehabilitation, dental, optical, hearing, speech, education, social services, mental

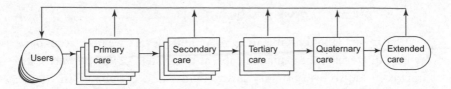

FIGURE 4.1   An Overview of the System

health, well-baby care, and immunization. Individuals would not be required to use the primary care facilities located in their community; they would be free to use any one they wanted.

Women coming to a primary care provider for prenatal care would receive ten dollars (or some other appropriate amount) for each authorized visit to either that provider or a specialist designated by that provider. Parents or guardians of children brought in for essential immunization would receive ten dollars (or some other appropriate amount) per visit per child. These payments would be covered by the community health care board.

A new type of health care professional, a primary care nurse-practitioner, would be created. This practitioner would fall between a registered nurse and a physician and would be able to treat some relatively uncomplicated ailments and prescribe treatments for them. Such primary care nurse-practitioners might well be trained as registered nurses but with an additional residency requirement. The primary care nurse-practitioner would be directly or indirectly supervised by a certified primary care provider.

Employment of such primary care nurse-practitioners by primary care providers would enable them to accept a larger number of patients and thereby increase their income. The nurse-practitioner would be paid by the primary care provider. Only the primary care physician could receive payment for vouchers received. A primary care nurse-practitioner could serve as a patient advocate and case manager.

In areas in which a primary care physician is not available, the responsible community health care board could certify a nurse-practitioner, enabling that person to serve as a primary care provider. This nurse would be subject to indirect supervision from a primary care physician designated by the board. That physician would receive extra compensation for providing such supervision.

SECONDARY, TERTIARY, AND QUATERNARY CARE

Patients would be able to enter a higher-level care unit (secondary, tertiary, quaternary, or extended care) at the system's expense only if authorized to do so by a primary care provider or a designated surrogate. (Surrogates could be appointed or approved by the primary care provider when the patient is in a community other than the one in which the primary care provider is located, for example, if the patient is in an accident while traveling.) Care facilities would be responsible for communicating with the patient's primary care physician on all matters of specialist referrals and action. The patient's primary care provider would remain involved in all the treatment decisions even if a surrogate has been appointed.

Ambulance service would be provided in each community. Its cost would be covered by the health care voucher and paid for by the primary care provider.

Patients, families, and close friends would have access to information about possible outcomes, treatments, and alternatives, and they could participate in treatment decisions and any special educational or training sessions in which patients are involved.

All secondary, tertiary, and quaternary care units would require second opinions for all invasive surgery and any other potentially life- or ability-threatening treatment if the treatment is outside the parameters of standard practice. Second opinions should be provided by physicians selected by persons other than the ones giving the initial opinions (e.g., the community health care board). Providers of second opinions should *not* know the identity of the providers of first opinions.

Whenever primary care providers so desired, they could ask for a second opinion from someone they select. In the case of a conflicting second opinion, a third opinion could be sought. Whenever there are conflicting opinions, none of which have been made by the primary care provider, that provider would participate with the patient in making the treatment decision. Physicians who choose to be part of the system would agree to provide free second and third opinions up to a certain number per year.

Every secondary and tertiary care unit would have a medical audit board, at least half of whose members would not otherwise be connected with the unit, and no more than half of whose members would be members of the medical profession. However, they would be qualified professionals and laypersons. The board would conduct audits of the quality of all medical services provided by the unit and would do so at least annually. It would report its findings, positive or negative, in writing to the community health care board. After a specified number of citations for unsatisfactory practices, a practitioner or service organization would be subject to review and reevaluation by the certifying body. This body would conduct audits of any practitioner or service organization within its jurisdiction for whom such an audit has been requested along with supporting evidence of the need for such an audit.

When a practitioner or service organization is subject to a series of successful malpractice suits, the cognizant auditing board itself should be reevaluated.

Secondary and tertiary care units should enable all technically trained personnel other than physicians—for example, nurses and paramedical personnel—to use as much of their knowledge as possible. At the same time, such personnel should be discouraged from regularly engaging in activities that could be performed by others who have less education and training. This would also apply to extended care units.

Quaternary care services would employ the most advanced technology and personnel and therefore be asset-intensive. Facilities to provide these services would service a larger area than tertiary care facilities, but they could be provided at selected tertiary care centers.

EXTENDED CARE UNITS

Authorized extended care would be provided to all those requiring it. The primary objective of extended care units would be to return patients to their homes as soon as possible. However, patients would not be released without permission of their primary care providers. Payment for extended care services would come from an authorization by the primary care provider requesting the community board to issue a voucher for such services to the person needing them.

Those living in extended care units would be provided with opportunities to engage in as many normal activities as possible. In addition to attending college and university classes on or off campuses, the residents might operate day care centers and provide tutoring and literacy training to others in their community.

All publicly supported institutions of higher learning should be required to allow residents of extended care facilities and senior citizens to attend classes at no or token cost, and their faculty members should occasionally provide courses at extended care units.

Units providing extended care services would be responsible for coordinating their activities with the primary care physicians of their patients. In addition, each resident of an extended care facility would have an admitting physician who would be responsible for coordinating medical decisions and consulting the resident's primary care provider. When it is apparent that the patient will never be able to leave the care facility alive, the admitting physician could be made the primary care provider if the patient or those responsible for the patient agree.

Wherever possible, the individual's home or the home of a family member or friend would serve as the extended care facility. The services required would be provided in the home by skilled personnel and their semiskilled assistants operating out of residential extended care organizations. Family members or friends would be trained to provide appropriate services whenever this would be desirable and feasible. Hospice care for terminally ill people would be provided by all extended care units, either "in house" or within private homes.

The Health Care Mall

Individual and groups of primary care practitioners could operate in facilities of their own or out of health care malls where population density makes them feasible (see Figure 4.2). Malls could be located in academic or corporate campuses or facilities or other places where there are concentrations of people.

The Wellness Subsystem

Along with the health care voucher, the national internal revenue service would issue a debit card acceptable *only* for wellness-producing and maintenance programs conducted by organizations certified by the community health care board. These organizations would receive pay-

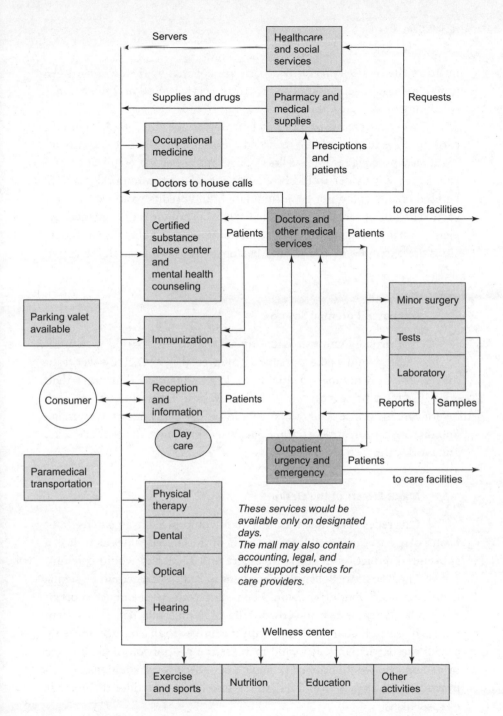

Servers

Healthcare and social services

Supplies and drugs

Pharmacy and medical supplies

Requests

Occupational medicine

Prescriptions and patients

Doctors to house calls

Certified substance abuse center and mental health counseling

Doctors and other medical services

to care facilities

Patients

Patients

Parking valet available

Minor surgery

Immunization

Tests

Laboratory

Consumer

Reception and information

Patients

Reports

Samples

Day care

Paramedical transportation

Outpatient urgency and emergency

Patients

to care facilities

Physical therapy

Dental

These services would be available only on designated days.
The mall may also contain accounting, legal, and other support services for care providers.

Optical

Hearing

Wellness center

Exercise and sports

Nutrition

Education

Other activities

FIGURE 4.2 The Health Care Mall

ment for the services they provide that are covered by the debit card. An individual could get a complete record of services used and the balance remaining on the card, if any.

Wellness credits would not be transferable (i.e., used for illness care) because they would be recorded on each individual's card. Any individual who engages in a wellness program under the cognizance of a primary care provider would be eligible for a health care tax deduction. Unused credits could not be accumulated, and credits would start anew each year. Social services, designated types of immunization, mental hygiene, nutrition counseling, family planning, and membership in fitness clubs are examples of what could be considered wellness-related activities.

Estimated Potential Savings

It is virtually impossible to estimate the savings that the system described here would make possible (Rovin et al. 1994). However, estimates based on numbers available in 1994 suggested that more than enough would be saved to cover all those not currently covered with health care insurance. Our system would reduce incidence of overpricing and unnecessary treatments, fraud, defensive medicine, malpractice suits, and work care.

Major Effects of the Design

Our redesigned health care system would provide an extension of health care coverage to all legal residents of the United States as well as a substantial reduction of costs. Medicare and Medicaid would be eliminated. The role of the federal government in health care would be significantly reduced. Employers would be required to cover only the cost of work-related health care and costs of illegal immigrants. The new system would be entirely market-driven with incentives to discourage abuse by any of the participants. It would increase the proportion of health care providers who would provide primary care—because it would make such practice more attractive and lucrative—and it would reduce the number of specialists.

The system would provide health care services to areas currently underserved, and it would encourage use of the system by many of those who should use the current system but do not. It would also encourage the formation of integrated health care systems and would promote health at least as much as it would treat illness and disabilities. Therefore, it would reduce national illness and disability care costs and losses incurred because of illness (e.g., absence from work).

POSTSCRIPT

In 1994, during the frenzied and futile attempts to reform the U.S. health care system by Congress and the administration, a group of people engaged in their own redesign effort. The participants included patients, nurses, physicians, pharmacists, administrators, and representatives of the insurance industry, the corporate world, and government. A monograph entitled *An Idealized Design of the U.S Healthcare System* detailed the outcome of their effort (Rovin et al. 1994). This chapter is a condensation of that monograph.

5 Education

Men are born ignorant, not stupid; they are made stupid by education.
Bertrand Russell

It is widely acknowledged that the public educational system of the United States has been deteriorating for several decades. This indictment also applies to so-called higher education. Despite sporadic, local experiments that offer promise, the system as a whole continues to go downhill. One report about elementary and secondary education is perhaps the most telling:

> The biggest piece of international research on educational standards, involving schools in forty-one countries, was published recently. It compared scores of thirteen-year-olds in math and science tests, calibrating the scores so that a mark of five hundred was equal to the international average. In math, as it happens, America's score was five hundred, placing it twenty-eighth in the league. England's score was 506, giving a rank of twenty-five. The Czech Republic, with 564, achieved Europe's highest score and a rank of six. At the top of the table was Singapore, with 643, followed by South Korea, Japan, and Hong Kong.
>
> The Czech Republic spent a third as much per pupil as did the United States. Many of the most generous spenders achieved results that were mediocre or worse. (*The Economist* 1997, p. 15)

In 1993 almost half of all Americans between the ages of twenty-one and twenty-five were estimated to lack basic literary skills, and there is no reason to believe the situation is better now. Because of the failure of the educational system, an increasing number of parents are opting to educate their children themselves or to send them to private schools. The poor state of the educational system cannot be attributed to any one problem; it is a *mess*, our term for a system of interacting problems that must be treated holistically or systemically if it is to be treated effectively (as discussed in Chapter 1). The problems of education do not exist in a vacuum, and they cannot be remedied by treating them as isolated from other social and environmental problems. Education is closely linked to the issues of poverty and welfare, crime, housing, and health care, to name a few. Education is amenable to substantive improvement only through a systems approach.

Education as a Creative Institution

To understand it properly, the educational system should be viewed as an institution that has certain social functions. Like all institutions, education helps to maintain the current integrity of society, to preserve the status quo. It is necessarily conservative. As a result, it fails to transmit to students the changing norms, values, skills, and understanding required to succeed in the emerging environment—in part because it neither knows what the requirements are nor understands the need for them. The educational system, screaming, resists being dragged into the new age.

A basic requirement of moving into a new age is creative thinking. But schools stifle creativity, particularly in children, by insisting that they conform to standards of behavior and belief, and by teaching them to respond to questions with answers that are expected of them. Answers that are expected cannot be creative, precisely because they are expected. Creative answers are necessarily surprising, unexpected. The current American educational system can be characterized as having students memorize known (expected) answers to predetermined questions. In an effort to please their teachers, students memorize predigested material selected by their teachers or others, material that fails to inform students about the changing nature of society and what the changes mean. Parents often reinforce the conservative efforts of teachers.

Students are also taught that certain questions must not be asked; for example, Jules Henry, a cultural anthropologist who argued that a humans' foremost evolutionary task is to learn how to learn, wondered what would happen "if all through school the young were provoked to question the Ten Commandments, the sanctity of revealed religion, the foundations of patriotism, the profit motive, the two-party system, monogamy, . . . and so on" (Henry 1965, p. 288). Ronald Laing (1967), an eminent British psychiatrist, answered that such questioning would produce more creativity than a change-resisting society could handle. The suppression of creativity continues when students graduate and enter the workplace, where they quickly learn that to maximize their job security they must give their bosses the type of answers expected of them.

Education is maximized when it is coordinated and integrated with work, play, and inspiration. These four functions are kept apart by institutions that are designed to carry out only one of them to the exclusion of the other three. For example, most places of work exclude play, inspiration, and learning; most recreational facilities exclude learning, inspiration, and work; and, of course, most educational institutions exclude work, self-determined play, and inspiration.

Most schools operate like industrialized disseminators of existing information that can be obtained, if and when needed, by other means. In schools that operate like traditional and now outdated factories, incoming students are treated like raw material coming onto a production line that converts them into a finished product. Each step in the conversion process is planned and scheduled, including work breaks and quality testing. Few concessions are made to the animated and purposeful nature of the students processed. Although students vary widely in quality, their treatment is uniform. The production process is considered to be successful if the final product is in demand and can be sold at a high price. The system even puts brand names and model numbers on its products and prints them on certificates and diplomas.

The pedagogy used would be appropriate if students were black boxes whose outputs were an exact reproduction of what was put into them. What most educators expect of most students can be delivered better by computers and recording machines. They hardly touch on what humans can do better than computers—think and act creatively. Students learn this with devastating effect; they abdicate responsibility for learning (which they equate largely with memorization) to computers and such. Computers can remember and recall, compare, and calculate more quickly and accurately than human beings can. But they cannot forget as easily as people can. Teachers forget that forgetting, unlearning, what is irrelevant or incorrect is at least as important as remembering what is relevant and correct. The overabundance of irrelevant information creates a much more serious problem than the shortage of relevant information because the amount of time required to filter out irrelevant information leaves less time for absorbing what is relevant.

Students should use machines as an adjunct to learning rather than being an adjunct to the machines. Students must be in control of the machines, not the reverse. Students should learn to do what machines cannot do or cannot do well. However, students cannot learn how to do what machines cannot do in a system that treats them like a product to be worked on and put together on an assembly line called a "curriculum." Formal education at all levels has been reduced to a number of discrete, disconnected parts. It is dissected into teaching and teachers, schools, curricula, grades, subjects, courses, lectures, lessons, and exercises. Artificial quantification and qualification are used to reflect the system's concept of the amount and level of what has been learned: grades, credits, diplomas, and degrees. Formal education is seldom if ever treated holistically, nor is it thought of by educators as part of a larger learning process, most of which takes place out of school.

Unless students subsequently unlearn (1) a great deal of what they learned in school and (2) what they have learned about how to learn, they are seriously handicapped. This is a consequence of the false assumption that being taught is the best way to learn. To the contrary, it is often the worst way; teaching is a major obstruction to learning. Of necessity, we begin our redesign of education by changing the focus of education from teaching to learning.

The Redesign of Pedagogy

Oscar Wilde wrote, "Education is an admirable thing, but it is well to remember from time to time that nothing that is worth knowing can be taught." Pedagogy is commonly taken to be the art of teaching. It is also defined as adult-directed instruction aimed at children. The implications of these definitions is that someone other than the learner knows what ought to be learned and how. We argue to the contrary.

We begin by noting what should be obvious: much, if not most, of what today's students will need to know and understand after they leave school cannot be predicted. We cannot predict all the significant additions to the information, knowledge, understanding, and wisdom that will become available. Furthermore, the rate of technological change will continue to increase. Such changes will augment an already considerable tendency of high school and college graduates to switch fields after completing their formal education. Jobs for a lifetime are things of the past. Most people can expect several or more jobs of differing content during their lifetimes, jobs that require continuous learning.

Even when graduates remain in the field in which they were educated, they need to replace and add to a major portion of their school-acquired knowledge in order to maintain their effectiveness. For these reasons, it is essential that graduates from schools at any level be ready, willing, and able to learn continually after leaving school. Because of the increasingly rapid obsolescence of what is learned in school and the increasing tendency to switch fields after graduation, what is learned in school is not nearly as important as learning how to learn and being motivated to do so continuously. Most learning takes place out of and after school—for example, one's first language and the skills employed at work—and it takes place without being taught formally.

Learning, learning how to learn, and being motivated to do so continuously can be accomplished in a number of ways, no one of which is the most effective for every student and every subject in every environment. The individuality of students requires access to a variety of learning experiences. There are many ways of learning that are more effective than being taught. Moreover, the effectiveness of pedagogical processes varies significantly with educational level, as well as with individual differences. Here are some of the alternatives.

BEING TAUGHT VERSUS LEARNING

Teaching, in contrast to being taught, is a very good way to learn a subject. Teaching others encourages and enables students to learn on their own and consolidate what they have learned. This is common knowledge especially among those who have taught a subject that they themselves have not been taught. All students, then, should be given the opportunity to teach others. While at first glance this does not appear to be feasible, there are ways around the apparent difficulty.

At the primary level, second-grade students can and have been used effectively to teach those in the first grade; students in the third grade used to teach those in the second; and so on. This was done with considerable success by Mary Rees, an innovative "teacher" at the Oak Lane Country Day School located in a Philadelphia suburb. In a sense, this is not much of a deviation from what happened in the old one-room schoolhouse, where the task of the teacher was to facilitate the teaching of students by more advanced students.

In high schools and higher levels of education, small groups of students (no more than ten) can be organized into learning cells in which they teach each other parts of one or more subjects. Being taught by a fellow student in a cell is very different from being taught by a teacher in a classroom. When a fellow student is involved, it is apparent to the "student" that the "teacher" is also learning. Learning then becomes a cooperative process in which the "student" has as much responsibility for helping the "teacher" learn as the "teacher" has to help the "student."

The primary function of a "teacher," whatever the level, should be to facilitate learning how to learn and motivating students to do so. University faculty members, who rarely have been trained as teachers, frequently have to teach subjects they were never taught. Similarly, graduate students who teach in colleges and universities normally learn a great deal more than do those they teach. They learn much more from this teaching than lower-level teachers who teach the same subjects over and over again. Teachers who change what they teach periodically impress upon the students the importance of learning how to learn. Being taught how to teach, as is done in colleges of education, is not a particularly good way to learn how to "teach." Teaching clearly cannot be done without making learning meaningful and fun, and inspiring.

COMPUTER-ASSISTED LEARNING

In education, computers are used predominantly to teach students. This is even worse than being taught by a person, because it is demeaning. However, computers can play an effective educational role as learners. By current standards, a computer is a perfect student; it remembers exactly what it is told and only what it is told, and it does whatever and only what it is told to do. This makes it possible for students to learn a subject by teaching it to (programming) a computer. Clearly, this is more easily done for some subjects than others, for example, arithmetic and algebra. Second-grade students at the Hawken School in Cleveland successfully learned arithmetic by teaching it to a computer, and they did so faster then those taught the same material by a teacher. It made the students feel superior to the computer, providing them with a good dose of self-respect, dignity, and pride in having mastered the beast.

Computers can be and have been used to facilitate learning in another way, for example, learning English grammar. Three personal computers equipped with light pens were arranged as shown in Figure 5.1. The students could see each other but not the screens facing the other two. The computer addressed the same question to all three. For example, "Point out the incorrect word in the following sentence: 'The people was at home.'" Students answered using the light pen. The computer then told them how many had given the right answer. If all were correct, it moved on to the next question, but if one or more were wrong, the computer told them that at least one was wrong but not how many or which ones. The students had to determine who was in error through discussion or by use of a resource (for example, a teacher) and make new entries. This process would continue until all the answers were correct. Note that the computer was used here to facilitate learning, not to teach. It also made learning fun and helped students develop communication and social skills.

In some cases the computer can be used to simulate a problematic situation and make learning by practice possible. For example, simulators are commonly used to train airplane pilots, aircraft designers, and naval engineers, and they do so very effectively without a high cost of errors. They are, in effect, a substitute for on-the-job training.

These examples by no means exhaust the possible uses of computers as aids to learning. Once we get over the desire to automate teaching, many effective educational uses of computers can be developed. In none of them should the student and computer be pitted against each other. The computer should be used as an instrument of the learner, not as an instrument used by others on the learner.

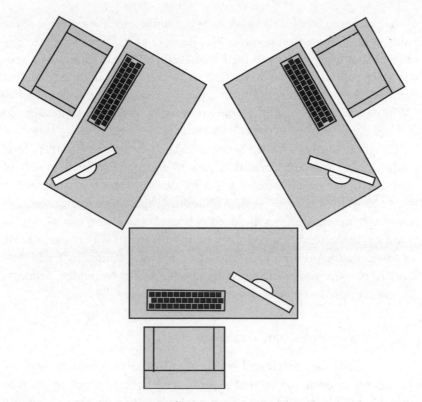

FIGURE 5.1   An Arrangement of Computers to Facilitate Learning

LEARNING THROUGH DISCUSSION (SEMINARS)

A great deal can be learned about a subject that is neither well developed nor well defined through discussion between students and others who have thought deeply about the subject. These discussions should be concerned at least as much with developing meaningful questions as with providing answers, and as much with developing the underdeveloped aspects of the subject as reviewing what developments there have been.

Another advantage of discussions between those who know or have thought about a subject deeply and those who haven't is that the latter can occasionally bring an insight or new thought or question to the discussion that doesn't occur to "experts" because of the "baggage" they carry into the discussion. Persons proficient in a subject often have more difficulty bringing a fresh perspective to it than do novices. Thinking "out of the box" is easiest for those who are not in the box. An example of the value of such discussion involves a series of conversations facilitated by one of us with students from the fourth, fifth, and sixth grades of a Sunday school about their dissatisfaction with their instruction. One student made a comment in the form of a question during these discussions: "Why do we have to hear the same stories each year?" The question led to a significant change in the curriculum.

At the Sudbury Valley School in Massachusetts, elementary level students have conversations; they talk to one another as a matter of course. There it is recognized that people develop their minds by talking (Greenberg 2000, pp. 47–48). At Sudbury, open communications between and among students and faculty is encouraged and stimulated because it is recognized that conversation is an essential way of exchanging meaning, learning by tapping into other people's minds. In traditional schools, open communication is discouraged, if not forbidden. Students are not supposed to talk in class unless spoken to by the teacher.

RESEARCH CELLS AND PRACTICUMS

Students are motivated to learn and best learn how to learn in solving real problems under real conditions with the guidance of one who knows how to learn and has done so under similar conditions. They can do all this in research cells and practicums. These cells should consist of no more than ten students working with one or more faculty members on real problems in the environment and, where possible, with the participation of those responsible for doing something about it. There is little as conducive to learning as awareness of the possible significant use of what is learned.

Apprenticeship remains an extremely effective way of learning. Medical practicums and residencies are universally considered to be more important in the education of physicians than attendance at classes. More great architecture has been created by architects who learned their trade through apprenticeship than by listening to architects in class. Music is frequently taught this way, especially to very young children, who learn to play an instrument by ear, observing and copying a teacher, or experimenting with the instrument, long before they learn to read music or understand the theory behind musical composition.

INSTRUCTIONAL COURSES

Instructional courses should include studios, laboratories, and experiential learning. They should be used to develop skills—for example, surveying, design, drafting, and crafts. They should also be used to develop understanding about living and functioning in the real world. Students would be evaluated in these courses for their ability to demonstrate understanding in their terms, not those of the teacher, and to apply the skills they have learned in the real world. An impressive example of this kind of instruction is the approach to early childhood education in Reggio Emilia, a city in northern Italy. In this publicly supported school system, children ages three through six, under the supervision of teachers, explore their environment by doing projects and expressing themselves about what they learn through various means, including words, movement, drawing, collage, sculpture, and music. For example, students are taken to a large neighborhood supermarket, where they interview the managers, observe the market's design, and actually shop. When they return to school, they express verbally and graphically what they have learned, including designs for packaging products, and they discuss adding facilities to the supermarket that would appeal to their age group (Edwards, Gandini, and Forman 1995).

INDEPENDENT LEARNING

If they desire, students at any level should be encouraged and allowed to learn any subject on their own, however they see fit, which is the way most of us learn most of the time. Independence is the vehicle of self-paced learning. The requirement that all students in a given class proceed at the same pace cannot be grounded on educational or learning principles. In a class of, say, thirty students there may be thirty different levels of ability and inclination to learn. Yet all thirty typically are forced to go at the same pace. The absurdity of this is clear: administrative convenience takes priority over the application of sound learning principles. Why else is "education" carved into defined blocks of time, for example, fifty-minute classes, fifteen-week semesters, four-year degree programs, and so on, when nowhere in the educational research literature can one find even an inkling of evidence to support the effectiveness of these divisions?

Individuals learn well when they go at their own speed and can choose what and how they learn, that is, when learning is individualized. The one-educational-size-fits-all way of thinking doesn't work; it never did and never will. Admittedly, it is more difficult to arrange educational programs and experiences for individuals than groups. But this is a how-to-do-it, a means-problem, and thus lends itself to solutions, many of which are already available. (The use of computers and the Internet, the Sudbury and Reggio Emilia examples at the lower levels, the graduate equivalent exams for those who have not completed high school, and the self-paced dental curriculum at the University of Kentucky in the early 1970s are examples.) It is not an ends-problem, because the goal is one virtually everyone accepts in principle, if not in practice: maximizing learning for everyone.

LECTURES

At least at the secondary and higher levels of education, faculty members should be able to give lectures that students should be able, but never be required, to attend. Attendance should be without credit. (Under these conditions, attendance is the best possible kind of feedback of the students' perceived value of the lectures.) The best lectures should be videotaped and made available through school libraries. Videotapes of lectures by outstanding faculty of other institutions should also be available to students and faculty. It is better to see and hear a good lecture on tape than a poor one in person. Those who have watched a good lecture can then meet face-to-face with or without a faculty member to discuss what they have been exposed to and through discussion consolidate their learning from it.

The Content of Education

One of the principal aims of education should be to equip students to treat previously unencountered problems, how to respond to the unexpected, appropriately. Students seldom learn that there are four very different ways of treating problems that were briefly discussed in Chapter 1: absolution, resolution, solution, and dissolution. While absolution, resolution, and solution are by far the most common approaches to treating a problem, we believe that dissolution is the most effective approach. Absolution, resolution, and solution are concerned with eliminating symptoms, which is temporary. For example, collective bargaining, as mentioned in Chapter 1, is a form of resolution, compromise, with neither side getting what it really wants. The dispute, symptom, is settled in the short term, but the cause, distrust between labor and management, is not diminished in the long run. Taking an aspirin usually gets rid of the symptoms of a headache, solution, but not the cause.

To dissolve a problem is to redesign either the entity that has the problem or its environment in such a way as to eliminate the conditions that cause the problem and enable the entity involved to do better in the future than the best it can do today, in a word, to "idealize." Flu shots generally eliminate the chances of getting the flu by preventing viruses, the cause, from taking hold; at the same time, they also eliminate the need to find a way to treat the symptoms.

The educational system should see to it that students learn how to design problems out of existence. Design is a creative act, one of synthesis, putting things together, not analysis. Most educators are unaware of the difference between analysis and synthesis, and how to design creatively. Creativity requires the identification of constraints (usually self-imposed), removing them, and exploring the consequences of having done so. Schools provide little opportunity to learn how to think this way.

PROBLEMS, EXERCISES, AND QUESTIONS

Problems are choice situations in which what is done makes a significant (value) difference to the decision maker. Exercises are problems from which at least some of the information required to formulate them has been withheld. Questions are further abstractions from problems; they are exercises from which the context of the problem and the reasons for wanting to solve it are usually not revealed.

Problems are not out there waiting to be picked, like apples off a tree. They are abstractions extracted from reality by analysis. They are to reality what atoms are to objects such as tables and chairs. What we experience are tables and chairs, not atoms; similarly, what we experience are complex systems of interacting problems, not individual problems.

This is why they have to be extracted, formulated. In school, problems are given; outside of school, they are taken.

Exercises are abstracted from problems which, in turn, have been abstracted from reality. The difference between a problem and an exercise is clarified by an example.

One of us was once given the following alleged problem by a friend: "You dip into a bowl containing black and white balls and pull out m balls of which n are black, hence (m – n) are white. Now, without replacing the balls you have drawn from the bowl, you dip into the bowl and draw out one ball at random; what is the probability that it will be black?" We told the friend we would answer his question if he told us how he knew the bowl contained only black and white balls. He said that providing this information would spoil the problem. We pointed out that, to the contrary, he had already spoiled it; it was not a problem but an exercise. He had omitted information on how he, or someone else, had determined that the bowl contained only black and white balls. Such information could be used effectively in estimating the probability asked for by my friend.

The case studies widely used in teaching, especially in law and business schools, are exercises, not problems. Their formulation leaves out much of the information required to formulate them. To be sure, the cases presented to students contain all the information that their authors consider to be relevant, and they leave out all or most of the information the authors consider to be irrelevant. However, they do not reveal the criteria used to differentiate relevant from irrelevant information. These criteria are critically important in problem solving. Good problem formulations and solutions often involve discovering that information initially considered to be irrelevant subsequently turns out to be very relevant. And this involves asking the right questions.

Some educators argue that what is learned in dealing with cases, even if they are exercises, is useful in dealing with problems. This is like arguing that learning how to box with one hand tied behind one's back is useful in learning how to box with both hands. In boxing, skill depends on the way one's hands interact, not on how each operates independently of the other. In dealing with problems, skill depends on the way different mental operations interact—for example, right and left brain—not on the separate actions of each. Effective problem solving requires systems thinking and asking questions about the system that contains the problem.

The example given in Chapter 1 involving double-decker buses demonstrates the importance of asking the right questions. In that example, what appeared to be irrelevant information to one person—the number of buses and stops in the system—turned out to be the key to the dissolution of the problem for another person. Case studies ordinarily do not raise the critical issue of what is and what is not relevant.

The principal difference between excellent and ordinary diagnosticians does not lie in the differences in the inferences they draw from the same information, but in the questions they ask to obtain additional information. The information they obtain through their additional questions reduces the probability of an incorrect diagnosis.

A question is an unmotivated exercise; it is a problem completely out of context. However, the reasons for wanting to answer a question determine what constitutes the right answer because these reasons give the context of the question. For example, the correct answer to "How many chairs are in a specified room?" depends on the use to which the answer will be put. Is a chair that requires repair before it can be used to be counted? If the reason for asking the question is to determine how many can be used right now, chairs needing repair or parts should not be counted. If the seating is not to take place for a week or more, then chairs that can be repaired within that time should be counted.

Even the question "How much is two plus three?" has no meaning out of context. The answer will not be the same if the "two" and "three" refer to degrees Fahrenheit as it would be if it refers to chairs. Two plus three on a logarithmic scale is six, not five; ten plus ten is one hundred, not twenty, on the binary scale; and so on and on. Learning how to answer questions is not the same as learning how to deal with exercises, let alone problems. And learning how to solve separated problems is not the same as learning how to deal with systems of interacting problems, what we call messes.

PROBLEMS AND DISCIPLINES

One of the greatest disservices of formal education is that, because of the way courses and curricula are organized, students are made to believe that every problem can be placed in a disciplinary container, such as physical, chemical, biological, psychological, sociological, political, and ethical. However, there is no such thing as a disciplinary problem. The world is not organized by disciplines in the way schools, universities, curricula, and courses are. Placing problems into disciplinary categories reveals nothing about their nature, but it does reveal the disciplines of the persons looking at the problems. The following story shows how approaching problems through disciplinary eyes does not yield satisfactory solutions.

A meeting of leaders of an urban black community and cooperating university professors (including one of the authors) was disrupted when a member of the community broke in with the news that an old woman who had been active in the community's development had just died. She had gone to the free health clinic in the neighborhood that morning for a checkup and had been okayed and sent home. On the third flight of stairs up to her rooms, she had had a heart attack and died.

The meeting stopped; all present were silent and contemplative. Eventually the professor of community medicine broke the silence by saying, "I told you we needed more doctors in the clinic. Then we would be able to make house calls and this would never have happened." After another pause the professor of economics said, "There is no shortage of doctors in the city, but they cost money and she could not afford one. If her welfare or health benefits were adequate, she would have been able to call a doctor to come to her." After another pause the architectural professor suggested that elevators be required in all walkups of four floors or more. Finally, the professor of social work said, "None of you seem to know anything about that woman. She had a son who is currently a partner in a major and very successful law firm in Philadelphia. He lives with his wife and children in a one-floor house on the Main Line [an upscale suburb of the city]. If she and he were not alienated, she would be living with him, have no stairs to climb, and have all the money she needed to call a doctor."

Clearly, the problem was not medical, economic, architectural, or social work. These were orientations from which the problem was viewed, similar to the parable about the blind men trying to describe the elephant, each from his own vantage point, and each incompletely. Nevertheless, problems tend to be placed into the same discipline as those who first identify it.

However, the best place to treat a problem is not necessarily where it appears. We do not try to cure a headache by doing brain surgery but by putting a pill in the stomach. Knowledge of how the organism works enables us to treat an ailment more effectively than we would otherwise. Nevertheless, students are not taught to look for solutions in places other than in the discipline of the one who identified the problem.

Complaints of occupants of an office building about slow elevator service were dissolved not by speeding up or adding elevators but by putting mirrors on the walls of the waiting areas. This occupied those waiting in looking at each other or themselves without appearing to do so. Then time passed quickly.

Students are not taught that there are usually many disciplinary points from which to view every problem and that until these are made explicit the best one (or ones) can seldom be selected. They certainly get no practice in using a transdisciplinary approach to problems—in discussing problems from a variety of perspectives.

PROBLEMS AND MESSES

Decision makers are seldom confronted with problems that can effectively be treated independently of each other. Instead they usually need to deal with situations that consist of complex systems of strongly interacting problems. As mentioned earlier, we call such situations messes. Students are not taught, and do not learn, how to deal effectively with messes.

A mess is the future we are now in, barring any change. It is the future implied by our current practices and behavior and the changes we expect in our environment. Such an implied future of every institution would show how it is on a path to self-destruction because it failed to adapt to (even expected) changes in its environment. What the projection reveals are the seeds of the self-destruction contained in its current practices and behavior. For example, the mess of the Federal Reserve Bank formulated in the 1970s showed that if nothing new were done the bank would eventually require more check clearers in the United States than there were people. It was awareness of such a crisis that led to development and propagation of the electronic funds transfer system. A more current example is in health care. At the current rate of increase of gross domestic product, now at 14 percent (Chapter 4), about 100 percent will be devoted to health care by the next century. Of course this is absurd! We can't and won't spend all of the nation's money on health care. But knowing where we are headed without significant intervention just might help us to make the appropriate changes and redesign the system.

One of the most important outcomes of education can be the understanding that solutions to problems can create worse problems than the one they are intended to solve. The failure to understand that problems are parts of messes often leads to solutions that do more harm than good—for example, prohibition, which was intended to reduce alcoholism, did not do so, and it stimulated and nurtured the growth of organized crime.

FROM DATA TO WISDOM: CONTENT OF THE MIND

Educational systems should distinguish between data, information, knowledge, understanding, and wisdom. These form a hierarchy with their value increasing as one moves from data to wisdom. Nevertheless, schools generally allocate time to these types of mental content inversely proportional to their importance. Most of what schools at all levels deliver is information, less knowledge, and virtually no understanding or wisdom. What is most unfortunate is that the students are not even made aware of the differences between these different types of content of the mind and the importance of the differences.

Data are symbols that represent the properties of objects and events. But they have little value until they are processed, converted into information. Information consists of data transformed so as to be useful in decision making. The difference between data and information is similar to that between iron ore and iron. Iron ore cannot be used to make anything; iron can. But iron cannot be obtained without iron ore.

Information is what is contained in descriptions: answers to questions that begin with such words as who, where, when, what, and how many. Knowledge is contained in instructions, answers to how-to questions. The product of knowledge is skill, ability to do something efficiently. Understanding is contained in explanations, answers to why questions. Understanding enables us to evaluate the relative efficiency of different bits of knowledge; that is, to determine what knowledge is relevant in a given situation.

Finally, wisdom is what is contained in value judgments, of the outcome of our actions—evaluated relative to their long-run consequences. Information, knowledge, and understanding are concerned with the efficiency with which objectives are pursued, but not the value of the outcome intended. Wisdom is preoccupied with the value to be obtained from the pursuit, with effectiveness rather than mere efficiency. Information, knowledge, and understanding are concerned with "doing things right," but wisdom is concerned with "doing the right thing." As we said in Chapter 1, the righter we do the wrong thing, the wronger it becomes. When the right thing is done wrong, it provides an opportunity for learning and improvement.

It is easiest for students to acquire data on their own, without help. It is not as easy for them to acquire information, but it is not usually very difficult. Knowledge is more difficult to acquire on one's own than data or information, and understanding even more difficult than knowledge. Wisdom, of course, is the most difficult to acquire without help. The help of an educated or experienced person is increasingly valuable as we move up the scale. Nevertheless, the educational system generally provides help only at the easy end—in acquiring data, information, and, to some extent, knowledge—and leaves students to fend for themselves when it comes to gaining understanding and wisdom. Little wonder! It is very difficult for educators to transmit what they do not have.

Value judgments are matters of ethics and aesthetics, topics omitted from most curricula. No learning should take place without consideration of the value of what is learned. No question is more important than "So what? What difference does it make?"

ERRORS

There are two types of error: (1) errors of commission; doing something that should not have been done; and (2) errors of omission, not doing something that should have been done, lost opportunities. Evaluation of students, as discussed in the following section, focuses almost exclusively on errors of commission. This carries over to social institutions in which lost opportunities and who is responsible for them are not identified. Herein lies the principal reason for the resistance to change shown by adult decision makers within organizations. The only mistakes that are detected and punishable are errors of commission. This means that doing nothing is the best way of avoiding doing the wrong thing. Unfortunately, this is the most likely way of failing to do the right thing.

To succeed in our society means keeping identifiable failure and errors to a minimum, and the foolishness of this precept goes unchallenged. One learns nothing new from being right; being right only confirms what one already knows, what one already has learned. Being wrong and trying to correct the error makes learning possible. We are not preaching the desirability of failure or the deliberate making of errors. We are urging greater tolerance for failure and error on both individual and societal levels because we cannot advance without it. Tolerance for error is especially important in our schools because this is where mindsets about error are formed.

The process of trial and error—trying new ideas and pursuing opportunities—is a critical part of learning, which is necessary for development. But identification of opportunities is not a part of learning in schools. Education emphasizes learning how to respond to what happens (reaction) or how to prepare for what is forecast or predicted (preaction). It does not emphasize how to make happen what one wants to happen (proaction) through design or how to respond to the unexpected.

Of course, the future must be taken into account in making decisions now, but these decisions need not be based on forecasts, most of which are bound to be wrong in an environment such as ours that is changing at an accelerating rate and becoming increasingly complex. The alternative way of dealing with an increasingly uncertain future is through assumptions. Contrary to popular belief, an assumption about the future is not a forecast. For example, we carry a spare tire in our automobiles even though we forecast that we will not need one on our next outing; we do so because we assume that it is possible.

Forecasts are about what we think is probable; assumptions are about what we think is possible. The difference between them is critical. We can take account of assumptions by contingency planning and maintaining flexibility—the readiness, willingness, and ability to respond to change. Many, if not most, plans that are based on forecasts are abandoned before they are fully implemented because most of these forecasts turn out to be wrong. Plans based on explicitly stated assumptions do not suffer from this possibility. Incorrect assumptions can usually be easily detected early, when the decisions based on them can still be modified appropriately without great difficulty or cost.

There is no better way to learn how to improve something than by redesigning it. Despite this, the educational process is devoted much more to research than design. Research, which is a necessary input to design, is concerned with the way things actually work, efficiency; design is concerned with the way they ought to work, effectiveness. (The difference between efficiency and effectiveness was elaborated in Chapter 1.) Acceptance of the way things are produces a population that tends to be satisfied with what it has and has little desire to improve it—and gives little or no consideration to how it might be improved. This is reflected in the Western world's current movement toward conservatism. Research alone cannot produce development; design is required for that.

Evaluation of Students

The principal purpose of an examination should be to stimulate learning, not to provide an evaluation. Conventional examinations—questions to be answered through multiple choice or exercises to be solved—should not be used to evaluate students, because these typically closed-book examinations do not model real situations in which competence is evaluated outside of school. Conventional examinations measure the ability to memorize rather than to think. At work, a boss does not have to subject subordinates to closed-book examinations to determine "how good" they are. Employees' abilities become apparent by working with them or watching them at work. Also, in most workplaces bosses expect subordinates to be able to use all relevant sources of information, knowledge, and understanding; in contrast, generally students are expected not to use any relevant external assistance. In real life, accessing these relevant sources, including collaboration, is a virtue; in the academic world it is called cheating.

More learning occurs by correcting mistakes than by reviewing what one has done correctly. When examinations are used, they should be repeated after students know what mistakes they have made and have had an opportunity to correct them. This would make it possible to determine how much they have learned from the examination. Regrettably, a preponderance of examinations are designed to make it impossible to learn from them because they are given after the fact, at end of the term or semester, when there is no class time left even to discuss the results.

An examination in which students are asked to formulate the questions as well as answers to them is much more revealing of what they know than answers to questions formulated by others. From personal experience, we can attest to the value of such exams in revealing the quality of student thought and depth of understanding. Further, all the faculty members who have contact with a student should meet periodically to formulate a collective evaluation of that student's overall performance. These evaluations should be reviewed with students by their advisers and placed in their record. Meetings with one's adviser should focus on ways the student can improve rather than what has been done wrong.

In the discussion of learning cells in which groups of students work together to learn through teaching each other, we mentioned peer evaluation, which is a natural concomitant of peer learning. It is taken seriously and is perceived as less threatening than that which comes from teachers. One of us oversaw an informal experiment in which students were evaluated on their ability to evaluate their fellow students' ability to determine quality of clinical care. The faculty made the same evaluations independently. Student evaluations were clearly as good as those of the faculty and were better received by those evaluated.

In brief, evaluation of what a student has done in the past should be replaced by efforts to improve what a student will do in the future.

Financing Education: The Voucher System

Much of social progress comes from a struggle for survival. This is as true for organizations and systems of organizations as it is for biological species. Public schools have not had to be concerned with survival because their survival is independent of their performance. They are subsidized and supplied with customers, most of whom have no other choice. All they need do is satisfy their subsidizers (governments and boards of education) and comply with regulations.

Christopher Jencks (1970), a Harvard education scholar, designed a system to overcome these shortcomings, the "voucher" system. (The version of this system that has been widely discussed and criticized by

politicians is a distortion of his concept.) Variations of this system are being used successfully in several communities. What follows is our own
variation on Jencks' theme, a variation that takes into account the major
unjustified critiques of Jencks' original design.

The parents or guardians of each school-age child would be given
an educational voucher worth a specified number of dollars payable by
the government to the school that receives it. This voucher would cover
tuition. An additional voucher to cover transportation would be provided
by the school with responsibility for the area in which the student lives if
that student attends a school outside of the area. This would provide an
added incentive for schools to satisfy the students and their parents who
live in the area assigned to them.

The vouchers could also be used to cover all or part of the tuition
to nonreligious private schools. (This would force competition between
the public and private system and, like competition in general, would
lead to better service of the system's consumers.) Parents could apply to
any nonreligious school for admission of their children. They would not
have to use the one in the area in which they live. However, schools
would have to accept applicants who reside in the areas assigned to them.
Admission of applicants who reside outside the areas assigned to them
would have to be made at random. (This would ensure equal access to all
applicants to any school out of their areas and make desegregation of
schools possible since race, religion, national origin, sex, or ability could
not be used as an admission requirement.)

Public schools would have no source of income other than what
they obtained by cashing in the vouchers they receive. Therefore, if they
did not attract and retain applicants, they would go out of business or go
into bankruptcy and be taken over by a receiver. The initial value of each
voucher would be equal to the average cost per student in the appropriate level of the public school system.

Private schools could charge whatever they wanted for tuition, but
parents would have to pay whatever they charged above the value of the
voucher. However, private schools would be eligible for receipt of funds
from vouchers only if they selected from among their applicants at random and offered a number (to be determined) of scholarships to those
families who could not afford to supplement the voucher.

This voucher system would encourage differences between

schools. Needed specialization would take place. For example, special schools or programs for deaf children or those with mental disabilities would develop, especially if vouchers for such children would be worth more than those issued for children without disabilities.

Introducing the market mechanism into the educational system would encourage its customers and consumers to become familiar with the alternative schools available. This system would foster greater parental involvement in children's education. Each community would provide information that would enable school users to make intelligent choices. In the system described here, individual schools would clearly be more responsive to residents of the areas assigned to them, more adaptive to changing needs, and more open to participation by their stakeholders.

Public education should be extended through undergraduate college and university levels. However, vouchers would not be issued for colleges and universities in the same way as for elementary, middle, and high schools. Anyone receiving a certified admission and registration statement from an institution of higher learning would be able to submit it to an appropriate government agency and receive a voucher that would defray all or part of the tuition required. But this would be in the form of a loan that would have to be paid back after graduation. Failure to do so would be treated as a very serious misdemeanor.

The voucher system is frequently accused of placing private schools under no obligation to accept or keep students that fall below their academic standards or become disciplinary problems. Clearly, the system described here is not subject to such criticism, because private schools that accept vouchers would have to select among applicants at random.

Faculty

All faculty members in any school would have the same rank and title. (This is intended to make each school a classless society.) Tenure would not be provided to faculty members, because it protects incompetence more than academic freedom, and there are more effective ways of protecting academic freedom. The initial appointments of those who have had no previous academic experience would be for three years. Subsequent appointments would be for six, nine, and twelve years. The final appointment would last until retirement. Initial appointments for those with previous academic experience would take such experience into account. For example, a person who has been in academia for ten years would receive a nine-year appointment, those with twenty years, a fifteen-year appointment, and so on. Each inexperienced new person would be assigned or could select an experienced person as a mentor. Finally, a mechanism would be developed to prevent those with long-term appointments (nine years or more) from abusing them (e.g., a brief review every three years). By abuse of an appointment, we mean intellectual retirement.

Academic freedom in each institution should be protected by a board of five members, two from other academic institutions and three from outside of academia, each appointed for renewable and staggered five-year terms. This board would hear any appeals concerning violation of such freedom, and its decisions would be final. Board members would have to be approved by a majority of the standing faculty members of the institution over which the board has jurisdiction.

At the college and university level, all faculty members would operate as profit centers. Their income would consist of a designated amount for each student credit hour they provide and the payments their departments receive for their time spent on research. Faculty members who incur annual losses would receive no increase in salary for the following year. Those who incurred losses for two consecutive years would not be reappointed when their contracts ran out unless they received executive approval.

The salaries of college and university faculty members would consist of a fixed and a variable component. The variable component would take into account their profitability, the amount of research they have brought to the school, and the amount and quality of their publications, all in the last year. At colleges where research is not a major requirement, the amount and quality of faculty effort with students would receive greater weight. The fixed part of their salaries would be approximately 75 percent of their market value.

Faculty members should be evaluated annually or biannually by (1) the students who have worked with them that year, (2) their peers in their departments and in the programs and research centers in which they have participated that year, and (3) the heads of these departments, programs, and research centers. Each year the department's chairperson would review with each faculty member his or her evaluations, and these evaluations would be made a matter of record and used in determining salary and status. Renewal of a contract would require approval by a majority of the members of a faculty member's department and a majority of the students currently in the institution who have studied with that faculty member.

Academic Facilities

In most academic facilities faculty offices are arranged much like cells are for monks. The privacy and inaccessibility of faculty members is maximized. Informal interactions among faculty members and between them and students are minimized. Nevertheless, such informal interactions, as the architecture of most schools preclude, can be very valuable learning experiences for both faculty and students. Faculty offices should be arranged around a court with glass walls separating the offices from the court. The court should have a lounge area in which students and others can wait for a meeting or meet with others (see Figure 5.2).

Schools, particularly public schools, are among the least well used public facilities; they are in use for only about 20 percent of the time. They should be designed to serve as community centers, including facilities that make them usable in evenings and nights and on weekends. The facilities can be those currently found in recreational and health clubs and clinics, and offices for heavily used public services, for example, issuing of licenses or tax information. The proximity of many active adults during school sessions would be a calming and steadying influence on students. Furthermore, by placing schools near or adjacent to such public service facilities as police and fire stations, calming and steadying influences would be further increased and opportunities for using these services in learning experiences would be enhanced as described earlier for the Reggio Emilia school system (Edwards, Gandini, and Forman 1995). Such design would also more closely approximate the real world mixture of people of all ages.

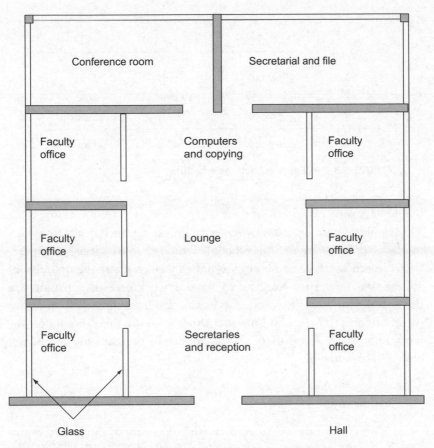

FIGURE 5.2   A Basic Enclosed Unit in a University

Academic Schedules

The academic year at all levels would be divided into trimesters, each fifteen weeks long. There would be two two-week breaks and one three-week break between trimesters. (With air-conditioned and heated schools, there is no reason to have long periods off.)

College and university students not employed on a continuing basis by a research center or as learning assistants would study during two trimesters and engage in required relevant work (paid or voluntary) for the third (see Figure 5.3). As a result, institutions of higher learning

	TRIMESTER		
	1	2	3
YEAR			
1	Study	Study	Work*
2	Study	Work*	Study
3	Work*	Study	Study

* Work for college and university students. Vacations for others.

FIGURE 5.3   A Trimester School Schedule

would have only two-thirds of their student bodies in session at any time. This would require significantly fewer facilities than such institutions currently have. Furthermore, this schedule would enable college and university research centers and other external as well as internal employers of college and university students to have a workforce of constant size throughout the year. It would also enable students at each level above those entering to orient and instruct those who are their juniors on the work to be done. A version of this could also be designed for upper-level high school students.

Summary

Criticism of the so-called educational system of the United States proliferates. Numerous reasons are given for its deterioration, including student alienation, lack of parent involvement, inadequate funding, violence in the schools, and quality of teaching. Each of these reasons has its champions, either in the form of self-organized groups of individuals or a formal organization. As a result, educational problems are addressed separately rather than as a system of interacting problems that should be dealt with as a whole (as explained in Chapter 1). And therein lies the mess. The dilemma of education is a systemic concern, a mess, not an aggregation of separate problems. Unfortunately, the educational establishment is taking a piecemeal rather than a holistic approach to the mess it is in; whatever changes it makes are incremental and small and consequently do not significantly change the system.

Schools act mainly as information and knowledge disseminators.

They value conformity more than creativity. The success of students depends on how well they memorize, not on how well they learn. But most of what they memorize is forgotten quickly unless it is applied to real situations. Schools seldom connect to the real world and especially to the larger learning process that occurs outside the schools. When students leave school, they are soon confronted with the uncomfortable need to unlearn the way they learn, not to mention a great deal of the content. We believe that the fundamental reason for all of this is the focus schools place on teaching rather than learning.

Because of the transient nature of information and knowledge, the accelerating rate of change in our world, and its increasing complexity, the emphasis of education should be on learning how to learn and being motivated to continue learning over a lifetime. What the system currently does is train students to be passive receivers rather than active learners.

We have offered several alternatives to current school practices, including having students learn by teaching as well as by being taught, using discussion groups that are aimed at students asking good questions rather than the current practice of seeking answers, independent and individualized study, practicums that enable students to grapple with problems of real relevance to them, and a choice of, and how they are exposed to, lectures. We would have teachers and peers evaluate students for how well they teach as well as learn. None of this is fantasy; everything we suggest has been used successfully.

We have introduced competition within the educational system and within individual schools. We have done so in order to make them more responsive to the needs of those they serve and less protective of the shortcomings of those establishments and individuals who pretend to provide service.

The basic ingredients of learning are (1) a desire to learn and (2) skilled and caring facilitators of learning who recognize that the learners' interests should come before their own, that conformity and creativity are not the same thing, and that creativity is the greater of these—and that without fun and inspiration learning is an unpleasant chore.

6   Welfare

Poverty is no sin.

George Herbert

Welfare is not the same type of problem as health or education. It is an intended solution to a complex set of interacting problems. Welfare unintentionally has increasingly exacerbated the problems it is intended to solve. The complex mess that welfare attempts to address includes poverty, the dissolution of families, the degradation of public education including the decline of literacy, under- and unemployment, segregation, and discrimination. The need for welfare in a society is proportional to its malfunctioning in important ways, the most important being that a significant portion of its population lives in poverty. Consequently, the primary focus of welfare has been on alleviating poverty. Paradoxically, it has been alleviated in a way that contributes to the preservation of poverty, a way that makes it a transmitted or "inherited" condition. Dependence on welfare is passed on from one generation to another.

Welfare consumes wealth without producing any. It is also blamed, at least in part, for children born out of wedlock and fathers who assume no responsibility for the children they have sired. It is also blamed for one-parent families, drug addiction, and crime.

In an ideal society there would be no poverty, and no need for welfare. All but the very young (preschool children) who are mentally and physically able would be engaged in education, socially useful work, or self-supported retirement after a socially productive career, living off accumulated savings. Those who would not be able to care for themselves—for example, orphans, those who are mentally or physically disabled, those who are infirm—would be provided for and taken care of by family, friends, or humane institutions that are privately or publicly supported.

There will always be some who cannot take care of themselves and who have no one who can, or is willing to, take care of them. A humane society is obliged to take care of such people. It is also obliged to minimize the number requiring such care. Society should see to it that everyone who is able has access to sufficient education to become and remain able to support themselves and their dependents by engaging in socially useful work. Societies ought to be judged more for the way they care for those unable to care for themselves than for their military might or standard of living provided to the more fortunate.

Many aspects of poverty are not discussed or treated sufficiently, for example, illiteracy, teenage pregnancy, venereal disease, AIDS, and men who fail to take responsibility for their children. It is widely believed that discussing such conditions publicly encourages the proliferation of those conditions, that pretending they don't exist leads to their reduction. For example, most communities continue to disallow frank discussion of sex and contraception in schools. The reason given for this is the belief that such discussion would encourage the sexual behavior that it is intended to reduce. This excuse flies in the face of the fact that most of our young people already engage in sexual activities, and most do so without the knowledge required to make such involvement safe and "unproductive." Another example: many if not most teenagers illegally consume alcoholic beverages more than occasionally. When Anheuser-Busch produced a flavored nonalcoholic beer (Chelsea) that teenagers could consume rather than alcoholic beer, the company was attacked by neoprohibitionists for having introduced a "baby beer." The neoprohibitionists argued that such a product would seduce young people into subsequently drinking alcoholic beverages, ignoring the fact that most of them already were doing so. Society allows moral proclamations to ride roughshod over facts.

Welfare itself cannot cure the problems that produce the need for it, but it can reduce their effects. Disturbingly, it can also make them worse by making living on welfare an acceptable way of life. Essentially, the most we can hope for—until society can eliminate involuntary poverty—is to motivate those in poverty to find an alternative socially acceptable way of surviving. It is to this end that our design is directed.

Addressing the Causes of Poverty

In our idealized city, people who are poor or disadvantaged would not live in homogeneous enclaves, ghettos, that would isolate them and transmit poverty from generation to generation. In an ideal city everyone would live in economically, socially, and racially diverse and integrated neighborhoods and attend schools or work in places that are similarly heterogeneous and integrated. Ideally, there would be no poor people, but if there were, they would be the responsibility of the neighborhood in which they live, not some more removed and impersonal unit of government. This system would reduce, if not eliminate, segregation and discrimination, and the reduction of these would in turn reduce poverty. This practice would also reduce, if not eliminate, the faulty decisions and waste of resources that occur when a far-removed body legislates on behalf of a community without really understanding its needs (e.g., Congress passing a welfare bill for rural Alabama based on national data or an organization's advocacy).

Not all the causes of poverty are easily eliminated. Some are very complex and not well understood, such as chronic sickness, living conditions that bring the drug scene to the front door, the conditioning that comes from being born to impoverished parents and cultural bias (Kozol 1995). But lack of education and unemployment are two causes that can be addressed effectively by ensuring equal opportunity for education and work to all. Individuals should be able to choose the kind of education and work they want. These choices should not be made for them by government. Government should become involved in individual choice only when an individual's private efforts fail and the primary community or neighborhood where the individual lives fails to provide the help needed.

WORK AND WORKFARE

Recent legislation requires welfare recipients who are physically and mentally able to work to seek it. But this is a catch-22 because many of the jobs available to welfare recipients do not pay significantly more than what welfare pays, and when they work, their welfare benefits are reduced by the amount they earn. This is a major deterrent to welfare recipients seeking work. Unless working income is significantly greater than welfare benefits, welfare recipients have no incentive to seek work.

Those on welfare who go to work should obtain a higher income than they can under welfare. This can be ensured as follows: welfare recipients would have their welfare payments reduced by only half of what they earn; then their income would increase as their earnings increase until their welfare payments were eliminated. For example, suppose a person's welfare payment was one thousand dollars per month and that person went to work for one thousand dollars per month. The welfare payment would be decreased by one-half, or five hundred dollars, per month. Then the total income would be fifteen hundred dollars per month. When the person's earnings reached two thousand dollars per month, that person would no longer receive any welfare.

Society could easily provide productive work to the unemployed, including work that improves communal quality of life. There are a number of things that need doing in society that otherwise do not get done, for example, demolition of condemned housing, clearing empty lots and converting them into recreational areas, removing litter from the environment, removing graffiti, and providing assistance to older people otherwise not cared for. In addition, many on welfare could work as parking-violation police. They could learn construction trades and work to build low-cost housing and to rehabilitate houses in need of repair. They could supervise children's after-school recreational activities. There is no end to the socially useful activities in which otherwise unemployed people could be productively employed.

Workfare has been suggested as a solution to the welfare problem. It requires welfare recipients to engage in socially useful work in order to receive welfare payments. But, according to David Ellwood, "There is something fundamentally different about 'working off a welfare check' and working at a community service job. In the first case you seem to be working for free, in the latter you are being paid for your work" (Ellwood 1994, pp. 159–60). Employment, not workfare, should be provided to and required of those able to work. It should be a primary responsibility of society to find or create employment for those requiring assistance and to see to it that they perform satisfactorily. Unfortunately, this is more easily said than done.

INSUFFICIENT AND INADEQUATE EDUCATION

Students and undereducated adults would be encouraged to continue their education until they have a level of competence sufficient to engage in useful employment at a salary that makes financial independence possible. Those who drop out of school would be drafted into an "army" performing public works projects in which they would receive further relevant education (discussed below).

Welfare would be used to support continuing education of those who could not continue without financial aid. Education does not have to be in a classroom; it can take the form of correspondence courses, on-the-job training, schools without walls, apprenticeship, and tutorials that help people earn degrees. As mentioned in our discussion of education (Chapter 5), subsidies for higher education would be available but would be treated as loans (not gifts) to be paid back after graduation or leaving school.

All those on welfare who are functionally or completely illiterate in the native language (English in our case) would be required to take part in a literacy program. All educational institutions that enjoy freedom from taxation would be required to provide such programs. As an incentive, those who attend them would receive a payment on successful completion of the program. The expense to society would be more than justified by the reduction of the need for welfare.

Homelessness

Homelessness continues to a major social problem. Although programs and services to help homeless people expanded dramatically in the 1980s and 1990s, visible homelessness in many American communities does not seem to have diminished. Astonishingly, large-scale homelessness persisted through the end of the 1990s, a decade of almost unprecedented national prosperity. And the economic downturn of the past few years suggests that it may have increased since Martha R. Burt and colleagues' comprehensive study (2001).

Estimates of the magnitude of homelessness depend on how it is defined, and they vary greatly. Perhaps a more useful estimate is based on the increase in the number of homeless people in shelters and public places over time. In his book *The Homeless* (1994), Christopher Jencks estimates that between 1980 and 1990 this number increased by over 250 percent, and countless homeless people were unaccounted for in his data. More recent studies estimate the number of people who are homeless during a given year to be between 2.3 and 3.5 million, including children (Burt et al. 2001). Over a five-year period, about 2 to 3 percent of the U.S. population, 5 million to 8 million people, will experience at least one night of homelessness (Link et al. 1995).

Many communities provide those who are homeless with temporary shelter, medical assistance, and legal redress. Government-supported centers and private coalitions provide some homeless people with continuing care, for example, Mitch Snyder's Community for Creative Non-violence in Washington, D.C., and Chris Sprowall's Philadelphia-based Union of the Homeless. Efforts such as these have reduced the suffering of homeless people but have not reduced their number; we believe it continues to rise.

WHO ARE THE HOMELESS?

The problem of homelessness has supplied some grist for the media mill. It tends to treat the problem as one stemming from mental illness or addiction to drugs and alcohol. The press often identifies the homeless with skid row. For example, the January 1986 edition of *Newsweek* claimed that most homeless people suffer from chronic and debilitating mental illness. This allegation was made despite evidence to the contrary (Snow et al. 1986; Jencks 1994). In the comprehensive Urban Institute study (Burt et al. 2001), 20 to 25 percent of homeless people had some form of mental disease.

In the conventional view of the problem, most homeless people are believed to be solitary men, disproportionately African American, and between the ages of twenty and forty. The Urban Institute study (Burt et al. 2001) shows that 66 percent of those who are homeless are single adults, three-quarters of whom are men; 11 percent are parents with children, 84 percent of whom are single women; and 23 percent are

children under eighteen with a parent. African Americans are disproportionately represented among those who are homeless, but in absolute
numbers they equal whites.

Homeless people are widely believed to be able to fend for themselves within the subculture they inhabit. They are seen as victims primarily of their own internal demons. In 1986 the *New York Times* conducted a survey asking respondents to what they attributed homelessness.
Laziness was cited by 20 percent, drug and alcohol abuse by 20 percent,
bad luck by 19 percent, and pathological problems by 12 percent. At the
time, these attitudes were reflected in statements made by political leaders, including President Reagan, who argued that the homeless were in
that condition by their own choice, and Attorney General Edwin Meese,
who claimed that homeless people live on the streets simply because they
find it the least expensive way to live. But this view was not then and is
not now supported by the facts (Jencks 1994; Link et al. 1995; Burt et al.
2001).

In general, we believe, homeless people are seen by the press, the
public, and politicians as individuals who either have chosen to be homeless or are mentally deficient. They create a problem for society, but society does not consider itself to be responsible for the problem they create.
Helping those who are homeless is seen as an act of charity, not as fulfill-
ment of an obligation.

EXACERBATION OF HOMELESSNESS BY SOCIETY

Homelessness is more than the lack of a home; it is a lack of fundamental associations with others and social institutions. Those who are
homeless are disconnected and isolated within society. Although society
is not generally believed to be responsible for homelessness, it is seen as
contributing to its increase through (1) increased unemployment, in absolute numbers, (2) increased shortages of low-cost housing, (3) the ejec-
tion of patients from overcrowded psychiatric facilities, and (4) tighter eligibility requirements for aid to persons with disabilities.

Another factor in the problem of homelessness is the changing
(changed?) nature of the skills required by the postindustrial or informa-
tion-age society, which has greatly diminished the need for the industrial
worker. Many of those without skills related to a high-tech, information-

based workforce are deprived of opportunities to work, especially in jobs with a decent income. The disappearance of the industrial working class as part of the transformation from the industrial to the postindustrial society long ago was identified as a source of homelessness (Lasch 1972). The computer-based economy no doubt has increased the number of such "displaced workers."

Carolyn Teich Adams (1986) points out that the changing demography of inner cities is also a source of homelessness. While less costly housing units are disappearing, a larger share of the city's population is composed of new household types: childless couples, elderly people living alone, young singles, and single-parent families. These households generally have limited income; they need and can only afford modestly priced housing. This has resulted in the displacement of those with even less income, feeding them into the ranks of the homeless. "What is new is the gradual disappearance of the lowest rung of the housing ladder, as postwar manufacturing centers have been recycled into post-industrial service cities" (Adams 1986, p. 531).

It would be relatively straightforward to think about remedies if homelessness was just a matter of shortages of low-cost housing and low-skilled jobs. But, as we stated earlier, homelessness is a very complex issue. And part of this complexity includes society's disenfranchisement of some of its members and their consequent alienation and withdrawal from that society.

WHAT SHOULD BE DONE ABOUT HOMELESSNESS?

Obviously, in an idealized society, poverty and homelessness would not exist. What can be done to prevent them? First, those who are able to work would be required to do so and would be provided with adequate low-cost housing. If they refuse to work, they would be placed in the communes described in the next section. Those who could not work because of a mental or physical disability, including alcoholism or drug addiction, would be encouraged to accept treatment and humane institutionalization, unless a responsible party is willing to take them in.

Each community would provide those who pass through these filters and insist on living out of doors with an enclosed site where the homeless could "camp out," have access to showers, washrooms, toilets, and lockers, and be provided with sleeping bags, ponchos, and pup tents. These areas would be patrolled frequently by social workers and the police.

Dealing with the Intransigent

Those who are able but refuse to work or to continue their education would be required to enter a "public-works army" in which they would receive food, shelter, clothing, and a small allowance, but no other support. The communes that house this "army" could be located in what were once army camps or new campsites, and their work might well involve such public works as building levees, reforestation, eliminating dumps, cleaning waterways and beaches, improving or building roads, and maintaining, enlarging, and constructing schools. Job-related education would also be available within these communes. Those who become willing to work or go to school outside the compound could leave whenever they got a job or were admitted to an external educational program. The communes would help their members find external employment and educational opportunities.

These public works communes would not be prisonlike. They would encourage and facilitate self-organizing work teams and learning groups. The residents would be encouraged to create enterprises that might eventually enable them to support themselves. Successful enterprises would be permitted to move outside the commune. Assistance in such activities would be provided by a resident staff.

The able-bodied and mentally capable who refuse to work, to continue their education, or to live in these communes would not receive welfare. The principle here is that separation from society should be the price of refusing to be socially useful. Begging and living in the open would not be permissible.

Child Support and Child Care

If parents, single or together, were unable to provide a child with adequate physical, psychological, and financial support, the child would be removed from the parent (or parents) and placed in an approved humane care center or foster home. If an absentee father were involved, he would be expected to provide child support. If the father was employed, support would be obtained through a payroll deduction. If he was not employed, a welfare agency would be expected to find work for him. Failure of a father to provide support for his child would be treated as a criminal offense. A child without a parent of record would be taken care of in an approved humane care center or foster home until adopted.

We consider a child born to a mother who is younger than majority age to be at risk. In this instance, an approved agency or court-appointed person would assess the status of the child and the likelihood of the mother (if single) or the parents to provide adequate care and support. If such assessment was negative the child would be removed as described above until the parent or parents could show the capacity for adequate care. Fortunately, there are both governmental and private services that enable at-risk children to get care and education and, in some instances, enable their parents to get training as parents at the same time and in the same facility.

The "Family School" in Philadelphia is an example of a program for parents and their children. "Kaleidoscope," also in Philadelphia and funded largely by Head Start, is a program for kids ages three to six whose programming is inspired by the Reggio Emilia approach in Italy described in Chapter 5 (Edwards, Gandini, and Forman 1995). In communities where such facilities are available, those facilities would be used first, before removing children from their parents. Also, services would be created that provide assistance to these young parents either from specially trained people (some of those in the work programs described earlier could be trained for this work) or from relatives who would receive stipends for their help. Older Americans, as described in the next section, might help as well.

Day care facilities and services would be available for working parents or those attending school. Any child under eighteen who is not being adequately cared for would be entered into a publicly or privately supported boarding school. They would be free to visit their homes on weekends or holidays and to receive visitors at other times. These boarding schools would be like English boarding schools that children of the affluent attend. Some such schools exist in the United States, for example,

Girard College, the Hun School, and Lawrenceville. The American Association of Boarding Schools provides a complete listing of those currently available.

Ironically, our society looks the other way when parents impose limits on a child's aspirations because of the inability to improve their socioeconomic status. Hypocritically, we find mental abuse of a child by the parents acceptable, but not physical abuse. We take physically abused children away from their abusers but do not do the same for those who are mentally abused or whose aspirations and expectations are depressed by them. A parent or guardian who does not help a child develop mentally—to aspire to the limit of the child's abilities—should be considered to be guilty of a crime and treated accordingly. This practice might discourage teenage pregnancy and one-parent families.

As we suggest in the next chapter, parents or guardians of a minor who commits a crime could be held responsible and receive the same punishment as the minor. This would encourage parents and guardians to actually know what their children are doing and who their children's friends are.

A minor should be able to apply to a court for a divorce from his or her parents. To be sure, doing so should require appropriate evaluation by social workers who specialize in parent-child relationships. Those separated from their parents should be located in a suitable place until they reach maturity.

Activities for Older and Disabled People

All tax-free educational institutions should be required to open their classes to senior citizens and to disabled people (for or not for credit). There would be a community center within walking distance of all urban residents and easily accessible to those living in rural areas. They would offer continuous educational and recreational programs for the elderly, as well as for others. As previously noted, these might well be in public school buildings (see Chapter 5).

In each community there should be a registry for retired persons in which they identify the skills they have that they are willing to use in helping others who are retired. Then their skills could be bartered for others that they need. For example, a carpenter might help a retired lawyer build a bookcase and in return receive legal or tax advice. Those willing to provide home health care, shopping, cooking, driving, and so on would be of great value. Retired individuals could also provide services to people who are not retired, for example, helping disabled individuals, providing baby-sitting, and providing child and animal care, tutoring, and house-sitting services.

Since the designation in 1935 of sixty-five as the official age of retirement for purposes of receiving social security benefits, life expectancy for men has increased from sixty-two years to more than seventy-three years, and it is higher for women. The official retirement age should be raised by at least five years, only about 40 percent of the increase in life expectancy. Also, in 1940 an American could expect to spend 7 percent of adult life in retirement. In 1996, that figure is 26 percent and is increasing (Mathews 1996). This means that there is a large number of older people who could be useful in increasing the collective quality of life of others and, at the same time, increase their own.

Drug-Free Welfare

All those on the modified type of welfare described here would be required to submit periodically to testing for drug use. Those who are found to be users of addictive drugs and who cannot support themselves or be supported by others would be required to live in the "public-works-projects communes" in which treatment of their addiction is provided.

The government should make addictive drugs available at very little cost to those who are registered as drug users and at no cost to those who are receiving treatment and for whom the drugs are prescribed by a physician. Distribution of these drugs by other than government sources would be illegal and heavily punishable. This should significantly reduce drug-related crime and discourage new users. (Note that a cash-free society, as described Chapter 2, would make drug trafficking very difficult.)

Welfare for the Affluent

Social security is welfare for senior citizens. Currently, they must accept its monthly payments even if they do not need it. Here is a potential source of much-needed funds, for example, to support programs directed at removing the causes of poverty. Social security payments should be a decreasing function of income. For those with an income above a specified level, no payments should be made. *Need is the criterion used to determine eligibility for all other social welfare programs; it should be the criterion used to determine eligibility for social security as well.*

Summary and Comment

There are four principal changes in welfare incorporated in the design presented here. First, productive work directed at upgrading the quality of communal life—for example, improving or maintaining urban infrastructure—should be found for all those not otherwise employed but able to work. Second, those who would otherwise be on welfare and who go to work would earn significantly more than they would receive on welfare, thus producing a strong incentive to substitute work for welfare. Third, welfare payments, including social security benefits (e.g., disability and retirement payments) should be inversely proportional to income and zero when income exceeds a specified level. Finally, welfare or, more generally, care for those who are economically disadvantaged, would be the ultimate responsibility of the neighborhoods in which they live. These neighborhoods could assign responsibility to another level of government, but ultimate responsibility would remain with them.

Those who have abandoned society should not be abandoned by it. It is unconscionable that a society that is capable of producing enough wealth to eliminate poverty does not do so. Society's conscience remains intact because it places primary responsibility for poverty on the poor. When discrimination and segregation are pointed to as contributing to the disadvantaged state of poor people, the response is to point to the few who have risen out of poverty to succeed despite their origin. To be sure, individual effort can make a significant difference, but the lack of motivation to make such an effort is largely the result of what society has not done. Generally, explanations of complex problems lie in the system, not the individuals.

As a society, we do not behave as though equality of opportunity is an inalienable right of all. We do not even acknowledge this failure. For such equality to exist, there must be no correlation between the socioeconomic and demographic characteristics of parents and those of their children, including life expectancy. Using this definition, it is apparent that our society is rife with inequality of opportunity. The children of the affluent are much more likely to succeed than are the children of the poor.

Unfortunately, more attention has been given to ameliorating the suffering and discomfort associated with poverty and homelessness than to eliminating their causes. This is due in part to the visual offensiveness of poverty and homelessness to those more fortunate. They find the sight of those who are poor and homeless to be distasteful and embarrassing. When those who live in poverty are out of sight, they are out of mind.

The problems of poverty and homelessness are not the consequence of any one simple cause. They are at least partially due to the indifference of society and the passive acceptance of their state by many who are homeless or live in poverty.

7   Crime and Punishment

Punishment, n. A weapon which justice has almost forgotten how to use.

Ambrose Bierce

Few things affect our quality of life as much as crime and the sense of insecurity of person and property that it produces.

The United States has the second-largest percentage of its population in prison of any country in the West, second only to Russia. Yet it has one of the highest crime rates among nations. One reason for this apparent contradiction is that a released prisoner has a greater probability of committing a crime than he or she had before entering prison, and the crime is likely to be more serious.

"Law and order" has been a major political issue in the United States for decades. It has played a significant role in many elections for public office. For example, during the 1988 presidential election, the allegation by President George Bush that his opponent, Governor Dukakis, was soft on criminals is generally believed to have helped Bush defeat the governor.

Independently of the statistics on crime, there still is a pervasive belief that murders, sex crimes, and other violent crimes, particularly those committed by teenagers, domestic abuse, and molestation of children are increasing. Pressure for gun control, longer sentences, and in some regions capital punishment has also been increasing.

In most developed societies crime is treated as a social problem caused by the criminal. Because of this, it is assumed that, if criminals are apprehended, convicted, and imprisoned, crime will be reduced. This approach flies in the face of reality. Prison is more a school for criminals than a correctional institution. Furthermore, the low rate of apprehension and conviction of criminals makes crime a business that generally pays well. The prevalence of poverty, discrimination, and segregation drives many to crime, while deterrence of criminal behavior by young people has been lessened because of diminishing parental guidance and influence of church and schools.

If crime is thought of as evidence of a society's failure, then it can be treated as an opportunity rather than a threat. Crime points to those aspects of society that need correction. It also points to the need for developing more effective ways of treating criminals; the threat of prison is not a sufficient deterrent, and incarceration does not reform most criminals.

The treatment of crime as an opportunity rather than as a problem leads to the belief that justice should be concerned at least as much with protecting individuals from societal deficiencies as with protecting society against criminals, not that the latter is less important. If criminals are generally taken to be ones that society or some of its members have wronged, then the justice system should protect them from further abuse by society and its members, as well as protect society and its members from them. The criminal justice system should focus on the correction of society at least as much as on the correction of criminals. Punishment of either is ineffective; the transformation of criminals and society required must be induced in other ways.

None of this means that criminals should not be apprehended and treated accordingly. It means they should be treated not only as victimizers of others but also as victims of society if they are correctable, and as mentally ill if they are not. The amount and type of treatment that criminals receive should be a function of their personal characteristics and the nature of the crime they have committed.

Crime Defined

By a crime we mean an act that deprives one or more people of the ability to do something they want to do and would be able to do were it not for the act of the criminal; or compulsion, persuasion, or inducement of another or others to perform such an act.

This is not a legal definition of crime, but one that is developmental, because in effect it states that a crime is any act that obstructs another's freedom of choice. This definition implies that there is no such thing as victimless crime. An act that has no victim is not a crime, whatever else it is. Laws that make victimless acts criminal, infringe on human freedom, for example, an old law that prohibited heterosexual kissing in public on Sundays. Given our definition, most crimes are prohibited by law, but there are many victim-full crimes that either are not illegal or, although covered by laws, are not enforced. Discrimination and segregation are examples. Drug addiction is a cause of crime in our society because it induces crime against persons and property and often imposes a burden on others. Under some circumstances, gambling and prostitution also impose a burden on others.

Meanwhile, an entirely new type of victimizing crime is evolving, one based on computer technology. Theft and fraud, for example, have found a new vehicle in computer networks. These networks provide a very efficient way for selling scams because direct personal contact is avoided or minimized. Computer networks can also be used for more lethal purposes. They facilitate the purchase of guns and provide instructions on how to make bombs, including the nuclear variety. Terrorist and antisocial militias can operate unfettered by means of computers. Crime, like business, is undergoing a technological revolution.

TYPES OF OFFENDERS

Criminals appear to fall into three major nonexclusive categories:

1. Those who, without provocation, are a threat, or cause physical harm, to others, for example, by committing rape, mugging, or murder. Theirs are violent crimes. Others must be protected from such criminals.
2. Those who deprive others of their personal property or freedom, for example, through robbery, kidnapping, libel, slander, embezzlement, or corruption.
3. Those who reduce the quality of the environment shared by others, for example, by littering, producing graffiti, making excessive noise, and polluting air, land, or water.

Of course, one person may commit any combination of these types of crime. The way criminals are treated should depend on (1) the types of crimes they commit, (2) judgments of whether or not they can be rehabilitated, and (3) the frequency with which they have committed crimes.

Some crimes are committed under circumstances that may never be repeated, for example, stealing because of desperation. In such cases imprisonment is wasted, but requiring compensation for those who directly or indirectly suffered a loss because of the crimes or community service or both are much more appropriate sentences.

TYPES OF TREATMENT

There are several different ways criminals can be treated:

1. Deterrent (controlling): Such treatment is intended to prevent the criminal from committing other crimes. Deterrence can be either physical (e.g., incarceration) or psychological (e.g., threats of punishment for doing wrong or promises of reward for doing right).
2. Clinical (therapeutic): medical or psychological treatment that is intended to cure, reduce, or stabilize physical or mental illness, or eliminate a character defect that is believed to be actually or potentially responsible for self-destructive or antisocial behavior.
3. Supportive (protecting): Such treatment is intended to remove its recipients from antisocial influences that they cannot resist except at great cost or risk. It protects them from threats of harm and provides them with such physical and emotional care and support as they have been deprived of but need.

These types of treatment are frequently combined or used sequentially. Physical isolation should be held in reserve only for those who have repeatedly committed crimes that hurt others. The fundamental objective of the treatment of criminals of all types is to enable them to learn how to participate constructively in society at large—not punishment or revenge.

Treatment of Those Dangerous to Others

People should be protected from those who pose a danger. Those who are dangerous to whomever they come in contact with—for example, sociopaths—should be kept isolated except when being treated. But few who are dangerous to others are dangerous to everybody. These criminals usually can live in a criminal community without being a danger to one another. They can be provided with a full, satisfying, and productive life while being separate from those to whom they are a threat. Depriving such offenders access to society as a whole does not necessarily require denying certain others access to them. Such others as family or friends who desire access to offenders could have it. Extended visits could be made available to offenders who are cooperative members of the criminal community. Such visits could accelerate rehabilitation of offenders.

A community of dangerous offenders could be designed as follows. Offenders would have the opportunity to work for a living within that community. Compensation for labor should be the same within such communities as outside. This could enable them to support themselves and their dependents and compensate those they have harmed by their criminal behavior. They would pay for room and board and taxes, and buy the goods and services needed for normal living. Society at large would cover the costs of security and correctional programs.

A community dedicated to correction should have a sound economic base, producing goods and services that are in demand both inside and outside the community. Such production could be used to supply governments and individuals, particularly those in need, with goods and services they require. Private industries should be encouraged to open branches in such communities. Governments would contract with them to build and operate manufacturing and other facilities. This is already being done to a limited extent and with substantial success. Consider the following example:

> Since 1979, 320 inmates have worked at Brun's plants. The prisoners, who earn $4.25 an hour, or federal minimum wage, pay 45 percent of their wages to the state for such expenses as room and board and victim's compensation. The program has saved Kansas more than 71 million, making a tiny dent in the $20,296 per prisoner American taxpayers

spent on the prison system in 1991, according to the Criminal Justice Institute. (Wylie 1993, p. 29)

Incarcerated criminals should be able to save or invest part of their income. Those who haven't completed high school or college and want to should be able to do so through classes in the correctional community or through correspondence. Publicly supported colleges and universities should be required to provide extension programs in these communities. Enrollment, however, should be voluntary.

Psychiatric and counseling services should be available to offenders who could benefit from them. When offenders are judged no longer to be dangerous to others (by three independent judges), they would be freed, either to leave the community or to remain. "Corrected" in this context means that they are no longer believed to pose a threat to others and that they have the skills, resources, and opportunity required to reenter society as constructive members of it. In addition, they should have access to an environment other than the one that produced their criminality. Where possible, "corrected" criminals should be returned to better conditions and environments than those that helped produce their criminal behavior.

Communities of criminals should be governed democratically by their members with as much freedom to make decisions as is consistent with their physically restricted state. The communities should be designed and operated to make the offenders reluctant but not unwilling to leave as soon as possible. Those inmates who do not want to leave should not be required to do so, because this might induce them to commit another crime to regain admission. However, if they elect to stay, they should be required to cover *all* the costs involved.

Treatment of those who commit crimes within these communities should be determined by the communities' criminal members. There is no better way to learn the meaning and nature of justice. Noncriminal personnel who administer and maintain correctional communities should live within them long enough to appreciate the quality of life they provide. Obviously, such personnel should be free to come and go as they please. Inmates at Washington State Prison once designed their own community with the help of an architect-inmate, Don Anthony White. It has a number of similarities to the design presented here.

Correctional communities could be the locus of a number of experiments. New types of housing could be tried without the restrictions imposed by out-of-date building codes and union regulations. In particular, prefabricated units produced and assembled by inmates could be used for their own housing. Innovations in education, health care, environmental control, and almost every type of social service and facility could be tested in such communities. They could also be operated as experiments in participative democracy. They might well become model communities for "outsiders" to emulate. For example, the criminals who were banished to Australia by the British contributed significantly to the creation of one of the most advanced societies on earth (Farnsworth 1997).

To those who believe the objective of prison should be punishment, the design suggested here must seem outrageous. But we see no benefit to be derived from punishing offenders, because punishment has not been shown to be effective in either deterring crime or "curing" criminals. What we have suggested is a system that reduces the cost to society of treating serious offenders. It also provides them with an opportunity to contribute constructively to society even while incarcerated.

Treatment of Those Who Deprive Others of Their Property or Freedom

Offenders who deprive others of property or freedom could be placed in communities similar to those just described, but they should be given more personal freedom within these communities. For example, they could work with tools that would not be made available to those who have harmed others. They too would be required to provide restitution to their victims and would not be subject to release until they had done so. The length of their sentences would be determined by the time required to make restitution to the victim or victims. Restitution would be defined by the court that sentenced them. Work-release programs would be available for those considered to be "cured" but who have not yet completed the required payments to victims.

Treatment of Those Who Reduce the Quality of the Environment Shared by Others

Those who harm the environment in ways that can be corrected would not be incarcerated but would be sentenced to undoing the harm they have done to the environment. Those who have done irreparable harm to the environment would be treated as those who have deprived others of their personal property. The community affected by their crime would be considered to be their victim. The courts would determine the fine that the criminal would have to pay to the community before being released.

Treatment of Those Who Are Not Dangerous to Anyone or the Environment

Even if one assumes that most crimes are due to social conditions, it does not follow that every criminal has been damaged by society or is dangerous to others. Some crimes are committed in response to unique nonrepetitive sets of subjective or objective conditions, for example, some crimes of passion are of the first type, and political crimes may be of the second.

Those criminals who are judged no longer to be dangerous to others, their property, or their environment are best treated by removal from the conditions that induced their crime. Punishment in any form is not likely to have any positive effect on them. They should be required to submit to counseling but be permitted to function in society in a useful way.

This is particularly true of juveniles and young adults. They are frequently treated successfully by being placed in special homes where approximations to normal family life are created. Their family members should be encouraged to visit them, and if a social worker approves, they should be able to visit their families. They should be encouraged to work outside or attend school. When they have saved enough money to live on their own and are mature enough to do so, they could "graduate." But they should be required to return to periodic group counseling and support sessions. In some cases there is not even a need for assignment to a home other than their own; assignment to counseling for a specified period of time may be enough.

We can think of no better way to prevent and discourage crime by minors than by making one of their parents subject to the same treatment as is imposed on their progeny. After having committed a third crime, a juvenile would be separated from his or her parents and made a ward of the state, and the responsible parent would be treated as a delinquent.

VICTIMS OF CRIME

The most common victims of crime are those who can least afford to sustain the losses incurred. The government (local, state, or national) whose laws are broken in crime should provide insurance for victims of those crimes. The amount paid out by government to victims of crime would provide valuable feedback on the effectiveness of its laws and crime-prevention measures. It would also provide a reasonable basis for determining how much should be spent to prevent crime.

No matter what the conditions are that produce criminal behavior, criminals should be made responsible for the costs their acts impose on their victims. Wherever possible, criminals should repay the government or the appropriate insurance company for payments made to these victims. Failure to do so would itself be considered to be a crime.

Police

When crime is publicly recognized as a problem requiring attention, the first suggestion usually made by most politicians is an increase in the number of police. Such a suggestion is directed more at increasing the rate of apprehension of criminals than at preventing crime. Crime prevention has never been the principal focus of police efforts, even though their presence is intended to be and often does serve as a deterrent.

Consider what a preventive (in contrast to a punitive) police force might look like. Its members would have no power of law enforcement or arrest, but they could serve as witnesses to criminal acts. They would not be armed, but they would be conspicuously uniformed so that they could easily be seen and identified. They would cover neighborhoods *on foot* and get to know and be known by the residents. They would be assigned to a specified area and supplied an office and be required to live in the area they serve. They would be there to help people or to help them get help whenever it was needed. They would be expected to know and understand the conditions that breed crime in these areas and thus direct the activities of the appropriate agencies to correcting them. Their activity would be exclusively constructive—making their areas better places in which to live and work. For example, if they see minors being drawn into crime because of lack of parental guidance, they would take steps to remove those minors from their parents or guardians and to place them where they could receive the proper guidance.

On their nightly tours on foot, preventive police should be accompanied by two or more of the residents of the area being covered. It should be a responsibility of all able adults living in that area to make such tours periodically. When preventive police see criminality developing, they would take corrective action. But if apprehension or forceful intervention is required, they would call on regular police officers to perform it. Mobile phones would place them in immediate contact with these police.

Preventive police would be available at any time to anyone in the area assigned to them. They would be responsible for seeing to it that someone in their areas who is arrested knows his or her rights and receives proper legal aid. They would also assist the reentry of ex-convicts into their areas and see to it that people from their areas are treated properly by the police.

It is apparent that preventive police would require all the skills and training of a social worker and a group-process facilitator and leader, but their orientation would not be toward alleviation of suffering so much as toward the removal of its causes. Alleviation of suffering should be the responsibility of social workers.

In order to ensure their objectivity, the preventive police would have a different director than would the police, but both should report to the same public safety board. Training for entry into the two forces would be completely different. Members of either force would be able to apply for transfer into the other.

The functions assigned to preventive police here have been incorporated into the function of the regular police force in Singapore. These functions include helping the community solve problems and mobilizing the members of a community into helping themselves.

Law

As argued above, the presence of crime should be considered to be an indictment of society. Analysis of crimes should amplify the indictment and indicate what changes are needed. Laws that the general public does not respect do more harm than good because they invite widespread violations, which, in turn, undermine respect for the law in general. This was the case when alcoholic beverages were prohibited in the United States, and when in some cities "blue laws" severely restricted activities on Sundays. The current situation relative to marijuana is similar to the old one relative to alcohol. When a law is widely disregarded, analysis of the reasons why it is being disregarded offers an opportunity to improve society.

The military draft during the Vietnam crisis was another case in point. The morality of the draft law and an undeclared war were brought into question by conscientious objectors and draft dodgers. Many argued that there was no practical alternative to the draft, particularly when a nation is at war, declared or not. Not so, as Professor Ronald A. Howard of Stanford University argued:

> A fairly obvious use of the pricing system is in the manning of the armed forces. We should simply pay high enough wages and fringe incentives to volunteers to attract whatever number and variety were required by our military commitments; there would be no draft. Those members of society who had what to them were more desirable life opportunities than serving in the armed forces would be free to follow them. Since there would be no compulsion, every serviceman would have willingly accepted his lot and, consequently, could be expected to perform his duties with general enthusiasm and efficiency. Of course, the expense of such a military establishment would exceed present cost under the draft system. This cost would be passed on to all of society by increased taxes, thus sharing the burden of military service indirectly among all taxpayers. If the nation were to engage in an unpopular war, it is probable that the pay of the servicemen would have to be increased to attract the necessary number. The increasingly high expenses would serve as a very proper feedback on the true cost of the whole adventure. Conversely, a war that had the support of the populace would find many dedicated citizens who would serve for nominal pay. (Howard 1967, p. B-684)

Consider an example of how law breaking can be used to indicate where the law should or could be changed and how. Before the revolution in Iran, the cabinet minister responsible for consumer affairs put forth the following problem to one of us:

The state-owned tobacco industry was the second-largest source of income to the government, second only to oil. This nationalized company had a number of factories producing many different brands of cigarettes that were sold through government-licensed stores for the equivalent of fifteen cents to thirty-five cents per pack. The government also imported American cigarettes, which were very popular, and were sold very profitably for fifty-five cents per pack. But income derived from the sale of these imports was decreasing because of increased smuggling. Smugglers bought American cigarettes in Kuwait tax-free and brought them into Iran illegally on small fishing boats. They were then distributed to and sold by unlicensed street vendors for about fifty cents per pack, five cents less than the government charged.

In an effort to eliminate this illicit competition, the government offered a reward for information leading to apprehension of smugglers, but there was little response. As a result, the government considered increasing the reward. The question the minister asked was, What is the size of the reward that will maximize net government income from acquiring and selling American cigarettes?

We obtained an analysis of the flow of American cigarettes through the government's acquisition and distribution system. Then we determined the cost of each step and calculated the total profit obtained per pack sold by the government. We then did the same thing for the smugglers and found that although they sold the cigarettes for less their profit per pack was higher than that of the government. Their acquisition, distribution, and marketing were more efficient than the government's. We recommended that the government duplicate the smugglers' operations and pointed out that if it did it would do even better than the smugglers because some of the costs incurred by smugglers (e.g., bribery of public officials) because of the illegality of their operations might be eliminated.

Similar thinking led some of our states to legalize gambling, introduce lotteries, and levy excise (sin) taxes on alcoholic beverages and tobacco products.

We suggested (in Chapter 6) that addictive drugs be legalized and distributed and sold by the government. Because the government would be able to sell these drugs profitably at a much lower cost than do drug dealers, the involvement of organized crime in the drug trade would be reduced significantly, if not eliminated. (It is also argued that such legalization can reduce petty theft and burglary committed by individuals to get drug money.) Furthermore, the government's income from the sale of these drugs could be used to subsidize treatment of addicts. (This is precisely the same treatment currently proposed regarding tobacco.)

We believe that the government's imposition of a "sin tax" on tobacco while subsidizing tobacco farmers is irrational. Should not part of the proposed tax be used to convert tobacco farming into other activities that are at least as profitable as tobacco farming?

The argument against legalizing addictive drugs revolves around the belief that making them available legally and inexpensively would condone, hence increase, their use. But this could easily be prevented if government-supplied drugs could be obtained only by prescriptions issued by doctors. This would discourage new users and put old ones on record and make them more reachable for treatment. The cost of doctors' prescriptions for government-supplied drugs should be covered by health insurance (see Chapter 4).

Regardless of arguments pro and con, the evidence is that interdiction does not deter illicit drug use. Interdiction in the form of a constitutional amendment did not even put a dent in alcoholism. Taking the profit out of the system and reducing demand (the two hand-in-hand) are the principal means of reducing illicit drug use.

Laws that are frequently broken, particularly those that are broken with at least tacit public approval, should be reexamined and reevaluated periodically. This does not mean that all frequent offenses should be legalized—for example, drunk driving—but it does mean that the effort to develop more effective ways of dealing with the problem should be pursued.

Many laws remain in force after they are no longer useful and may even be counterproductive. All laws should contain a "sunset clause," that is, a specified date after which they would no longer apply unless reenacted. This would require periodic and systematic reevaluation of all laws (as was suggested above) and clearing the books of those no longer needed.

Finally, no amendments to proposed legislation, other than those relevant to the subject of the legislation, would be permissible.

The Courts

In addition to the function of interpreting the law and dispensing justice, the courts should be given the responsibility to evaluate and suggest improvements to existing laws and propose new ones for the legislature to consider. This means they should compare the performance of an existing law with the effects it was explicitly intended to have. Where there is a significant deviation between a law's performance and the expectations associated with it, the cause (or causes) should be determined and corrective action taken.

The performance of these functions raises the question of who should have this responsibility. We believe that neither the legislative nor the executive branches ought to be responsible for the evaluation of laws because they are the initiators of them. A possibility would be to give an independent body this role, but we don't want to create another bureaucracy. We believe the judiciary, because it has to interpret laws as part of its role in dispensing justice, is most suited for this responsibility.

This responsibility should be one of oversight and making judgments, not actually doing the required research and gathering information. The courts should be provided with (internal or external) researchers who are capable of carrying out the required monitoring, evaluation, and determination of effectiveness. Additionally, legislative bodies would be required to submit explicit statements of the expected effects of laws and regulations they enact and the assumptions on which these expectations are based. (In the best of worlds, legislative bodies would do so without a formal requirement.) Judges, on presentation of this documentation, would recommend corrective actions to the relevant legislators and regulators. This would enable legislators and regulators to learn how to make better decisions.

When corrective actions are taken by legislatures or regulators to amend or otherwise improve a law or regulation, a record of this would also be submitted to the court. These decisions and their implementation would also be monitored and diagnosed and corrected when appropriate. This would enable the courts to learn how to facilitate and encourage the learning of the decision makers.

The courts should periodically prepare summary reports of their evaluative processes and release them to the public. This would enable public pressure to develop when legislation or regulation fails to do what it is intended to do.

Courts should be held responsible for determining what social conditions are producing crime. Information of this type should be accumulated and analyzed, then made public and submitted to appropriate legislatures and regulators. In addition, courts, assisted by attorneys and researchers, should also be responsible for detecting new problems as they arise or, better yet, before they arise.

For example, consider the abortion issue. The dispute appears to be one of values, but it is not. The courts should point out that the difference between "right-to-lifers" and "right-to-choicers" is primarily a disagreement on the meaning of *life*. Both sides are not willing to kill living humans. The question is, at what point at or after conception can the product of fertilization be said to be living. The courts should be managing a public and legislative debate on this issue, not the so-called value issue.

Furthermore, there is an associated issue. When a fetus is known to develop into a seriously disabled or deformed baby, should it be aborted? When should current death be taken to be preferable to subsequent life? Where pets are involved, criteria are used that differ from those used when people are involved. Rational public debate of such issues should take place following the rules of debate set forth by Anatol Rapoport (1960) or as extended by Russell Ackoff (1974, pp. 108–11). A way of resolving confict is shown in the appendix.

In brief, the courts should provide much-needed feedback to legislative and administrative branches of government and to the public on society's actual performance. They should also provide feed-forward on potential future problems that can be minimized or avoided. This would facilitate more effective response to, and anticipation of, social threats and opportunities.

Special Kinds of Crime: Corruption and Terrorism

CORRUPTION

We single out corruption for special attention because it, perhaps more than any other type of criminal behavior, obstructs the development of a society. Although corruption is by no means restricted to less developed countries, it is certainly more overtly prevalent in them and more conspicuously obstructive to their development. However, even in well-developed countries corruption in government breeds cynicism among its victims and reduction of their democratic rights.

The following dictionary definition provides a reasonable grasp of what is popularly meant by corruption: "perversion or destruction of integrity in the discharge of public duties by bribery or favor" (*Oxford English Dictionary*).

Holders of public office are not the only ones who can be corrupt. Unfortunately, professionals and corporate managers have been known to indulge. So-called white collar crime can be as economically violent, if not more so, as the other types of crime are physically violent.

Immoral corrupt acts may or may not be illegal. For example, bridge toll collectors have been known to buy commuter books of tickets that reduce the cost per crossing of an automobile. Then when a person came through paying the full toll, the collector would put a ticket in the till and keep the difference. Although the amount gained per crossing may be small, the number of times the substitution was made resulted in a large sum of money being retained by the collectors. There was no law to preclude this behavior. Because it was considered inappropriate, a law prohibiting the practice was subsequently passed. The issues of insider trading and whether to put stock options on balance sheets are other examples of the indistinct boundary between inappropriateness and illegality.

Some election practices at all levels—for example, the way funds are raised and the use of misleading statements or outright lies about opponents—are immoral and inappropriate, if not illegal. To say that such behavior reduces the public's faith in and trust of government is a considerable understatement. It reinforces the view of many members of the electorate that voting is of no consequence.

Anticorruption measures are very difficult to take without the support of public opinion. Public indifference to, or tolerance of, corruption is a virtually insurmountable obstruction to the enforcement of measures directed against it. (Witness the reelection of Marion Berry as mayor of Washington, D.C., after his conviction for drug usage.) It is not surprising that some argue that corruption is what public opinion considers it to be and that it is not criminal, immoral, or inappropriate as long as the public tolerates it.

The greatest difficulty that arises from reliance on public opinion to define corruption—and there are a number of other lesser but not negligible difficulties—is its cultural relativism. For example, in seventeenth-century France the selling of public offices was considered perfectly legitimate. This is equally true today in some less-than-well-developed countries. For example, in India, Mexico, and many other countries, giving gifts and gratuities to public officials is considered to be a necessary and expected "courtesy."

Should such acts that are publicly tolerated or condoned be considered corrupt? Yes. It is desirable to have a definition of corruption that is not culturally relative, largely because corruption, whether publicly condoned or not, is a major obstruction to the development of any society (see Chapter 8).

Public tolerance of corruption is irrelevant to the question of its criminality, immorality, or inappropriateness, because our definition of crime is independent of legal and public opinion. The public's tolerance of corruption has no effect on its consequences, but public opinion does affect what is done about it. Corruption keeps government agencies from performing their functions fairly and efficiently, and this always has its victims. It can completely subvert development programs into ones that facilitate and increase exploitation of the disadvantaged by the privileged.

> Last May an internal Palestinian audit—which itself was rather slip-shod—claimed that the Palestinian government had squandered $326 million, or 400 percent of its 1997 budget, through corruption or mismanagement.
>
> . . . When a prominent Palestinian American journalist, Daoud Kuttab, tried to televise the legislative debates on corruption, he too was jailed. (Rubin 1997)

The Causes of Corruption

The root causes of corruption are *scarcity, maldistribution, and insecurity* as they relate to one's standard of living and the conditions that make up one's quality of life. Those who have little or none of necessary or desired resources are more easily corrupted. In some countries, survival may depend on acting corruptly. Corruption can work in both directions. Under conditions of deprivation, it is commonplace for those who do not have a needed or desired resource to bribe those who control its distribution so as to acquire some of it. For example, access to scarce goods was almost impossible in the old Soviet Union without bribery, and the same may be true in today's Russia.

Even where there is enough of a resource to go around, many may not have enough of it because of its inequitable distribution. Those who do not have enough want more and often act corruptly to obtain it. Those who have more than enough often engage in corrupt practices to satisfy their greed.

Where there is a scarcity of resources and maldistribution of what there is, those who have some or even enough of it often feel insecure, threatened. They want to protect what they have against potential loss. This is often "best" accomplished through corruption. For example, an employee who feels insecure about his job where employment is hard to get may give a portion of his salary to his boss in order to secure his job. Without scarcity or maldistribution of a resource, there would be no such insecurity.

Maldistribution produces scarcity, and scarcity produces insecurity. It follows that corruption could be reduced by (1) eliminating scarcity, (2) distributing relevant resources equitably, and (3) insuring possession of such resources against loss or appropriation. These steps are not imminent. What should be done about corruption in the meantime?

In the case of publicly provided services and resources, corruption can be reduced or eliminated by introducing a market economy into their distribution. Recall the breakup in Mexico City of the centralized licensing bureau, which had a terrible record of inefficiency, poor service, and corruption (see Chapter 2). It was broken up into small offices placed in each section of the city. The income of each office was derived exclusively from payment by the city for each license it issued. An office's income depended on the number and types of licenses issued. Those wanting a license could use any of the decentralized issuing points, which now, of course, were competitive. They could survive only by serving their customers well. Service quality increased, costs decreased, and corruption virtually disappeared.

Reduction of Corruption

In general, corruption in government can and should be reduced by the following measures:

1. Wherever possible, a service provided by government that can also be provided by private-sector servers should be opened for competitive bidding from both the public and the private sector. Contracts awarded should be effective over relatively short periods of time so that rebidding is frequent.

2. Where possible, consumers of a service should pay for it even if it is supplied by a public agency, and alternative sources of supply should be made available. Income from payments for service received should be the only source of income for the public-serving organizations.

3. Where it is not feasible for consumers to pay for a service, the provider should be compensated for services rendered, not subsidized by means of a budget that is independent of the organization's performance.

4. Since corruption is frequently a crime in which the public is the victim, those caught in the act should be identified publicly and disgraced. They should not be allowed to keep any of the gain they have obtained by their corrupt practices, and they should make restitution. Jail sentences, when appropriate, and heavy fines should be levied.

Corporate Crime

Corporate fraud is one of the most devastating sorts of crime because of the number of lives adversely affected by it. (In Dante's *Inferno*, fraud and betrayal are considered the worst of all the sins.) Witness the current spate of what is euphemistically called *malfeasance*, as exemplified by some of the executives of Enron, Anderson, WorldCom, and doubtless many others.

Laws have obviously not been significant deterrents to such crime. The federal criminal code in the United States currently includes more than three hundred fraud and misrepresentation statutes (Skeel and Stuntz 2002, p. 21). One might think that all these laws would have dissuaded some of these executives from misconduct. This is not to say that new laws and revisions or elimination of old ones are not needed. If history is any indication, enacting a lot of legislation will not change much in the long run. Some fundamental changes in the nature of corporations are required.

Corporations have traditionally been conceptualized as organisms. This is reflected in the fact that the word *corporation* derives from *corpus*, meaning body. We speak of the *head* of a corporation, its *health*, *sickness*, *birth*, and *death*, all biological concepts. The law treats corporations as individuals, as, for example, in the recent sentencing of the Arthur Andersen Company.

In our design, the corporation would ideally be treated as a community. In a corporation so conceptualized, there are no owners. "In a community the individual is a member, not an employee, a resource, not a cost, and is not easily to be expelled. Those who provide the investment needed get their fair return and their security, but they do not own it. No one owns a community, any more than one owns a family" (Handy 1999, p. 51). This change in the way a corporation is thought of would remove the excuse currently used by executives to manipulate corporate books: maximization of the value of the stock they and external shareholders own. This incentive would be further weakened if managers were prohibited from owning stock in the corporations they manage. Rewards for performance would take the form of bonuses approved by corporate boards.

The corporation's board should include membership of its employees drawn from all levels. They should be a plurality on the board. This would preclude executives benefiting at a cost to their subordinates.

Furthermore, the structure of a community is lowerarchical, not hierarchical (see Chapter 2). This means that those in positions of authority in a corporation would be selected by their "subordinates" *and* their "superiors." No manager would hold a position without simultaneous approval of the immediate superior and immediate subordinates.

Finally, pension funds should be insured either privately or by the government. These funds should not be allowed to "disappear" when a corporation has financial problems, even to the point of bankruptcy.

The principle that underlies this design is that employees have the greatest stake in an organization's performance. More than any other stakeholders they contribute to its success or failure, and they have the most to lose from its failure. Because of this, our design puts them in a position to exercise oversight, not alone, but in collaboration with other stakeholders who should also be represented on the corporate board.

Corporate executives convicted of criminal behavior should be sent to prison. They should be required to work with other inmates in establishing businesses that are run within the prison, as we described earlier, and to train others to engage in productive labor both in and out of prison. Corporate criminals should also be required to make restitution to those they have harmed, just as we have required of other criminals.

TERRORISM

There is an increasing amount of violent crime being committed not for personal gain or revenge, but in support of a doctrine, religious or secular, or a quest for freedom (in the form of the so-called freedom fighter). But regardless of motive, violence against the innocent is committed by terrorists, a special type of fundamentalist.

Fundamentalism

Fundamentalism is a response to an environment that is undergoing an accelerating rate of change and rapidly increasing complexity. These two conditions combine to produce what is generally referred to as a turbulent or chaotic environment. It is one in which it is easy for individuals and organizations to become disoriented. Fundamentalists respond to this environment with a prescribed set of beliefs about what are acceptable ends and means. These beliefs are taken to be absolute; they require unqualified adherence. No exceptions are allowed. The beliefs on which fundamentalism is based end the need for thought; they are based entirely on faith.

In brief, fundamentalism is based on a doctrine, normally formulated by a guru, which reduces the way of dealing with a complex environment to a prescribed set of actions and associated questions and answers. This set is considered to be sufficient for dealing effectively with the environment. Any questions or answers outside this set are taken to be meaningless.

Introverted fundamentalists want only to be left alone to practice their beliefs in isolation; for example, the Amish and Mount Carmelite nuns. Extroverted fundamentalists want either to convert nonbelievers (as missionaries) or to treat them as enemies to be suppressed or removed. Extroverted fundamentalists who accept violence as a way of affecting nonbelievers are terrorists. Not all fundamentalists are terrorists, but virtually all terrorists are fundamentalists.

Current Approaches

Retaliation for their attacks has only strengthened terrorists' resolve. It initiates a continuing tit-for-tat exchange that is characterized by increasing violence that has no visible end or resolution. The Israeli-Palestinian conflict and now the entry of the United States in its "war against terrorism" are examples. Johan Stumpfer, a professor from South Africa, in private correspondence wrote the following:

> I have followed the U.S. response to this problem with alarm. There is no way you [the United States] will succeed in getting rid of this problem with all the military might, financial might, and various responses I have seen so far. It will take a long time, because the United States is big and strong, but you cannot win this in the sense that the terrorists will be defeated. I grew up in a society structured around terrorism. I have seen this in my own country and other countries. You will not overcome this . . . unless there is a culture and value shift of enormous magnitude. You will contain it for short periods, but "getting rid of it" requires you to rethink your society.

Containment and isolation of terrorists have not been particularly effective because they do not weaken the terrorists' beliefs, for example, in Iraq, Libya, and Afghanistan. In fact, the containment and isolation strengthen their resolve because those that suffer by isolation, imprisonment, or death (as in suicide bombing) are portrayed as martyrs or victims of an evil force.

Terrorists cannot be contained or isolated as long as there are societies willing to tolerate them, let alone protect and provide them with the resources they require for their "work." Sanctions imposed on such societies do not reduce their resolve. Efforts to isolate, through sanctions, the nations that harbor terrorists have generally been ineffective because those who want to eliminate terrorism do not want to harm the innocent. Terrorists know this and tend to surround themselves with innocent civilians, in this fashion protecting themselves against attack. Where, despite this, they are attacked, as in Lebanon and Afghanistan, and innocent civilians are killed, this is used effectively in the propaganda war against the "enemy."

Because terrorism arises out of an inability to cope effectively with one's environment, there is a clear need to focus on education of the young, to produce understanding of their environments, the opportunities it presents, and how to take advantage of them. To our dismay, it is primarily in disadvantaged societies that such education is not provided and that terrorism is supported. The 2002 *Index of Economic Freedom* prepared by the Heritage Foundation shows that the countries that are the breeding grounds for terrorists are the least advanced economically. These countries suffer from inequitable distribution of wealth, opportunities for development, and quality of life. These conditions contribute to the frustration and alienation that give rise to terrorism.

Societies with a high standard of living, quality of life, and multiple opportunities for advancement are not likely to produce terrorists. Unfortunately, extreme and violent behavior is not precluded from even the most advanced societies, particularly those in which discrimination and segregation are pervasive. But even these conditions are not necessary for breeding terrorists. Witness some of those who advocate the "right to life."

Nevertheless, a reduction (if not the elimination) of terrorism from nations that are its principal sources requires the elimination of the maldistribution of quality of life, standard of living, and opportunities for a decent life. This is not being done by existing international organizations such as the International Monetary Fund and the World Bank. It requires a development-support strategy resembling the one used in a Philadelphia so-called black ghetto, Mantua (described in Chapter 8).

In the meantime, the current practice of capture and imprisonment of terrorists is not likely to reduce their inclination to engage in terror when released but is likely to increase their commitment to it. They need to be "detoxed." Their current treatment is not likely to accomplish this. We do not know how to do this. But we should be conducting experiments to determine how it might be done. It might well require putting them on an isolated island that is ceded to them with full sovereign rights, much as Napoleon was put on Elba in 1814.

The Cash-Free Society and Crime

Corruption and many other types of crime would be eliminated in a cash-free society (see Chapter 2).

> Imagine a society in which cash no longer exists. Instead, "cash" is electronic, as in bank-card systems. Currency and coin are abandoned.
>
> The immediate benefits would be profound and fundamental. Theft of cash would be impossible. Bank robberies and cash-register robberies would simply cease to occur. Attacks on shopkeepers, taxi drivers, and cashiers would all end. Purse snatching would become a thing of the past. Urban streets would become safer. Retail shops in once dangerous areas could operate in safety. . . .
>
> Drug traffickers and their clients, burglars and receivers of stolen property, arsonists for hire, and bribe-takers would no longer have the advantage of using untraceable currency. (Warwick 1992, p. 19)

It would be foolish to assume that such a system would be perfectly secure, but it would be even more foolish to assume it would not increase security and reduce crime significantly.

Summary

The usual approaches to dealing with crime, interdiction, and incarceration have not been successful because they are antisystemic; they address symptoms, not causes, and they do not include the interacting components of criminal justice: police, the law, courts, victims, and, above all, attributes and deficiencies of society. We are not absolving criminals of responsibility for their crimes, nor are we blaming crime on its victims, but we are saying that deficiencies in society lead to criminal behavior more than criminal behavior leads to deficiencies in society.

We have chosen to think in terms of treatment rather than punishment of the criminal because punishment has not proved to be effective as a deterrent. Retribution seems to us to be a major premise on which society currently bases its handling of the criminal. And while this may be a natural tendency, we believe that when possible restitution should be thought of before retribution. By restitution we mean it for both victim and criminal.

We suggest two types of police, preventive—working with people in communities to help prevent crimes—and police officers who function to apprehend criminals, much as they do now.

We believe that the courts should do more than dispense justice; they should evaluate and help improve the laws, because they are in the best position to do so: they see firsthand the effects of the laws and whether the laws are doing what was intended. Our laws, particularly those that are frequently broken, should periodically be reexamined and reevaluated for their effectiveness and usefulness. Adding a sunset clause to our laws would help to ensure this.

We treat corruption as a special case because it obstructs societal development more than other types of criminal behavior. Its root causes are scarcity, or the fear of it, and greed. An improved distribution of wealth and the introduction of a market economy in government (see Chapter 2) would go a long way toward reduction of corruption. The replacement of cash and coins by electronic transfers, that is, becoming a cash-free society, would go even further toward eliminating corruption and a large number of other types of crime.

Corporate crime (corruption) might be reduced by treating the corporation as a community, which by definition has no owners and is lowerarchical. This means that (1) corporate officials could not own stock and thus would have no incentive for manipulating the books, and (2) in a lowerarchy those that govern, management, would be subject to the approval of those governed, the employees.

Terrorists are fundamentalists who have zero tolerance for any belief system other than their own and believe that violence is the only way to achieve their ends. Their answer to the accelerating pace of change and complexity in the world is absolutism, and any deviation is not tolerated either among themselves or among others. The conditions that breed terrorists and foment terrorist violence are inequities in the distribution of wealth, quality of life, and opportunities for development.

While the capture and imprisonment of terrorists is essential, their violent behavior is not lessened by isolation or geographic containment; nor does retaliation dampen their zealotry. To the contrary, terrorists welcome the chance to call themselves martyrs.

While a high standard of living, quality of life, and abundant opportunities for development do not preclude terrorism, societies with these attributes are less likely to produce terrorists than are societies without them. At least one focus, then, should be on the reduction (if not the elimination) of the maldistribution of quality of life, standard of living, and opportunities for a decent life in those nations that are the principal breeding grounds of terrorism. Despite good intentions, this is not an approach taken by most existing international organizations. It requires a development-support strategy resembling the one used in Mantua, a so-called black ghetto in Philadelphia, which will be described in the next chapter.

8 Leading Development

Even trying to be helpful is a delicate and dangerous undertaking.

John Gall

Growth and Development

Growth and development, as noted in Chapter 1, are not the same thing. Neither is necessary for the other. A rubbish heap grows; it does not develop. On the other hand, many individuals (for example, Einstein) and less developed societies develop without growing. The opposite of growth is contraction, and the limit of contraction is death. Some cities and many individuals have developed while contracting. The opposite of development is not contraction; it is decline. (For example, in several aspects, such as distribution of wealth and social services, the United States is in decline.) Development, not growth, is an essential objective of societies. Growth can be justified only if it contributes to development.

The measure of a society's economic growth is the quantity of resources that it makes or helps make available for use, that is, the standard of living it provides. In contrast, development has to do with how well resources can be used and created in the pursuit of objectives. It has to do with what one does with what one has. It is better reflected in quality of life than in standard of living. It has to do with increases in an individual's or group's competence, which is a mental property; growth has to do with increases in physical properties, quantity. Robinson Crusoe is a better model of development than are the Rockefellers, Onassis, or Murdock. To restate:

Development is an increase in one's ability to satisfy one's own needs and "legitimate" desires, as well as those of others.

Needs and desires are not the same things. A need is something required for health or survival, like oxygen or food. People may or may not desire something they need—for example, they may not even be aware of their need for calcium or vitamin E and, as a result, not want it. On the other hand, they may want things that they do not need, such as addictive drugs, fatty foods, and ostentatious jewelry.

A legitimate desire is one that when satisfied does not reduce anyone else's chances of satisfying their legitimate needs or desires. Harming others (which includes depriving them of resources) is not a legitimate objective (desire) except when necessary to prevent them from harming someone else.

Development is a matter of learning, not earning. Then, since one person or group cannot learn for another, no person, group, or society can develop another. The only kind of development that is possible is self-development. This does not mean that development cannot be affected by other individuals or society; others and society can facilitate and encourage self-development. Good teachers do just this for their students, and good societies do this for their members.

The unattainable limit to development is the ability to satisfy all our needs and legitimate desires and all those of others.

Aspects of Development

Development has four aspects: the pursuits of (1) truth (through science, technology, and education), (2) plenty (through economics), (3) the good (through ethics and morality), and (4) beauty and fun (through aesthetics). The pursuit of each of these is necessary for development, but only when they are pursued together is continuous development possible.

The role of aesthetics in development is not as well understood as the roles of science, technology, education, and economics, or even ethics and morality. This is reflected in the fact that the terms *management science*, *management technology*, *management education*, and *management ethics and morality* convey some meaning to most managers. On the other hand, the *aesthetics of management* conveys little if any meaning to most managers.

The limit of development, its ideal, is *omnicompetence*, the ability to satisfy any need or legitimate desire. An ideal is an approachable but unattainable objective. The continuous pursuit of any ideal requires both inspiration and recreation. Beauty, whether produced by a human being or by nature, inspires; it produces an unwillingness to settle for what we have and a desire to create something better. Beauty is both a product and a producer of creative activity. Creativity is essential for pursuing ideals and continuous development. Art also recreates (entertains), yielding fun from what we do regardless of what we do it for. It provides the satisfaction we derive from "going there" in contrast to that derived from "getting there." Recreation provides "the pauses that refresh." It energizes the pursuit of ideals and provides payoffs along the way.

Stimulating Development

The major obstructions to development are cultural and political rather than economic or technological. The problem, therefore, is how do we bring about change in the minds that make up a society, minds that resist change with a strength that challenges even the best minds within and outside that society? The resistance to developmental transformations has two sources: first, those who benefit from the lack of development of their society—they resist any effort to improve for fear they will lose their privileges—second, those who cannot imagine the types of changes required to initiate meaningful development in their societies because of the lack of education and opportunity for improvement within their societies.

A government cannot develop its people; the people must develop themselves. This cannot occur until they want development, understand what it is, and know how to acquire it. They must be willing to invest at least their time and effort in its pursuit. The societal problem, then, is first to inspire people to launch a crusade for development and to facilitate its implementation, and second, to overcome the resistance of those who benefit from lack of development. Leadership is necessary on both counts.

Historically, crusades have been of two types: those directed *against* something, getting rid of what is not wanted, and those that are *for* something that is wanted. In other words, crusades try to undo or do something. War is the most common type of an undoing crusade. People have been willing to make unlimited sacrifices to destroy an enemy, or to undo the effects of such natural catastrophes as floods, earthquakes, and hurricanes. Dislike and hate have stimulated more crusades than have compassion and love. The only thing that appears to be able to bring about a crusade in pursuit of something wanted or loved is a mobilizing idea, an inspiring vision. Christianity, Islam, and democracy were originally such ideas.

IDEAS, NOT IDEOLOGIES

Ideas can do it. Ideologies can't. The right kinds of ideas cannot be found in ideologies, whether political, economic, or religious. Why? Because ideologies specify a set of means believed to be the only way to obtain a rigidly specified end. Ideologies consist of fixed ideas that do not adapt to different social conditions, different environments, or even different needs and desires. The rigidly specified means become ends in themselves and leave little room for choice. Recall (from Chapter 5) that without choice there can be no learning, and without learning there can be no development.

Even if one believes that adopting an ideology can promote development, which of the conflicting ideologies should be adopted? Conflict between ideologies is one of the most divisive forces in the world. Historically, it has been a principal cause of war. War is too big a price to pay for development; only affluent nations can afford it, and the price is excessive even for them. Their continuous preparation for war deprives less developed societies of the resources that could well jump-start their development efforts.

Ideologies focus on teaching, not learning; hence, they do not produce development. They promote unqualified acceptance of specified beliefs and attitudes, not knowledge, understanding, and wisdom. They reduce the ability of people to think for themselves, hence learn and develop. Those who want to initiate the pursuit of development do not need to provide a doctrine or a dogma but an opportunity for followers to develop by making choices that can have a significant impact on their standard of living and quality of life.

DEVELOPMENT AND TERRORISM

Earlier we described how terrorism might be combated through development, providing opportunities for people in countries that breed terrorists to use their innate abilities to pursue legitimate desires and advance themselves. This means having the opportunity and mind-set to make choices about their lives, including what and how they learn. By definition, the fundamentalist thinking that gives rise to terrorism (as described in Chapter 7) does not allow for choices about learning. It is extraordinarily difficult for adults in these circumstances (perhaps in any circumstances) to change how they learn and think, to *unlearn*, because unlearning requires the asking of questions and challenging assumptions about basic beliefs. (It is difficult, but not impossible. The Sufi Indians, for example, learn to think about the opposite, what is contrary to what they think they know, as a part of their education.)

On the other hand, young children do not have to unlearn because they have little to unlearn; their minds are not yet formed. This is where development efforts ought to be directed first, to kids. Programs should be developed that enable children from these areas to learn about other children and other ways of living. This won't happen in their existing school systems, with their current teachers. Any development resources given to underdeveloped countries should include as a requirement resources for exchange programs, for kids to live and learn with kids from other walks of life and for kids from other areas to learn with them.

EXTERNAL FACILITATION OF DEVELOPMENT

The initiation of development in a less developed society or community is not just a matter of more resources for the less developed. It is one of enabling the less developed to use whatever resources they have access to in a way they (not others) believe will most accelerate their development. This involves a concept of aid to a community that is illustrated in the case that follows.

Mantua. This Philadelphia neighborhood lies one-half mile to the north of the University of Pennsylvania. It consists of eighty city blocks and has an official population of about fifteen thousand, about 98 percent black. In the 1960s it was considered to be one of the worst areas in the city. Whatever standards were used, it was at or near the bottom of the list. As a result, it was frequently referred to as "the bottom."

Early in 1968, Forrest Adams, a resident of the community, came to the Busch (Research) Center of the University of Pennsylvania's Wharton School for help in preparing a public housing proposal to be submitted to the city. This help was provided, but he was asked to bring in the community's principal leader so that an unusual proposition could be put to him. The next day Adams appeared with that leader, Herman Wrice. The center offered to employ any three people Wrice selected from Mantua for work on community development projects of their own choosing. No constraints would be placed on how, when, or where they worked. They would not even be required to come to the university for any reason, but the center would offer any assistance the community requested.

Herman Wrice wanted to know "What's in it for the university?" We explained that we wanted to help the community develop but did not know how to do so. Hence, we hoped that with the arrangement proposed we could learn how to assist Mantua and in turn other disadvantaged communities.

The next day Wrice appeared with three Mantuans, two men and one woman. A few days after their briefing, the team asked for a meeting with the center's director. They wanted to review a plan they had prepared. In the course of doing so, they made twenty-one requests for assistance from the center. In addition, they asked for weekly meetings to review the center's efforts to fill their requests and to accept new ones. Before long more than thirty people from the university were involved in filling requests made by the Mantua team. Eventually, one staff member and a graduate student were assigned full time to the effort.

After about six months of collaboration, the Mantua team and the center prepared a proposal for continuing financial support of the community, not from the university but from both corporations and foundations. Such support was obtained, enabling the collaboration to continue. The following is a partial description of the project's accomplishments.

A black industrial park was established that employed about three hundred people. The center helped to establish and sustain a number of small businesses in the neighborhood. The community created an employment service that placed several hundred people in the first few years. Three medical facilities were established; none were previously available in the community. The neighborhood became actively involved in the management of the schools within its area, increasing their retention rate and admissions to colleges by their graduates. It created day nurseries and infant care centers, a special school to capture dropouts, and, with the collaboration of the Wharton School of the university, initiated an evening program in business and management that served about a hundred students each year. About half of those who attended subsequently entered evening degree programs at various local universities and colleges.

A training program for gang leaders was conducted at the university, one completely designed and controlled by the participants. Of the twenty-one who attended, seventeen subsequently obtained productive employment in city government and local companies, two went to prison for crimes committed before the course, and two disappeared. The community established a consulting service that helped private and public organizations deal with race problems. For example, it obtained an extended contract with the State of Pennsylvania for this purpose and managed to disarm every racial crisis that arose over the next few years, as well as finding equitable solutions to a number of corporate problems.

A number of recreational programs for young people were established. These involved all the major sports. Teams from Mantua won several city championships and traveled to a number of distant cities to compete with their champions. Academic competitions were also initiated, including a scholarship Olympics.

Most recently, under Herman Wrice's leadership, the community initiated an antidrug program, which it has subsequently replicated in about four hundred other communities across the country (*The Wrice Process* 1993). These have had dramatic success, reducing crime and drug traffic significantly. For this work, Herman Wrice received the America Award in 1993. His work has been the subject of two national television programs. He and his community have received numerous awards. Without his inspiring leadership, none of this would have been possible. But even with his leadership the development that took place would have been unlikely without the support of the university's Busch Center.

Unfortunately, while working in a community in Florida, Herman Wrice died suddenly a short while ago. A number of his followers under the leadership of his son, Tony, have continued his work. It has even been extended to communities in Africa.

What this case shows is that a group of skilled people—such as were provided to Mantua by the Busch Center in the Wharton School—with access to a wide variety of human resources can assist and accelerate development of a community providing they contribute only in ways that the community and its leaders see fit. This did not mean the center had to be completely passive. To the contrary, it continuously made suggestions and offered advice, but it never made a decision for the community.

PRINCIPLES OF DEVELOPMENT

Most developed countries believe that they understand development and that their understanding can easily be transferred to less developed nations. The same is true for the many nonprofit organizations that exist to help communities and disadvantaged groups. *This is a misconception* that must be replaced by realizing that developed societies and the organizations alluded to do not know how to eliminate underdevelopment. There is not a single instance of a more developed country being responsible for the elevation of a less developed country. For example, no colonial power ever produced a colony as developed as itself. Governments and "helping organizations" of more-developed nations and communities should stop acting as though they know how to develop less developed communities and societies. Development is not a matter of applying the technology and resources available in a more developed society to ones that are less developed. Technology is not culturally neutral; it can make a small minority of rich people richer, and a large majority of poor people poorer.

From another perspective, there are at least some less developed countries—but unfortunately not enough—that would like to avoid the very rapid and excessive urbanization, pollution, traffic congestion, crime, drug usage, and other disorders associated with development. If more-developed nations gave up the assumption that they can develop ones that are less developed, then they might be able to facilitate and encourage the self-development efforts of the less developed without passing on the negative aspects of more developed societies.

Many of the students from less developed countries who go to more-developed countries for education do not return to their homes, not so much because they are attracted by a higher standard of living (although this has an effect), but because they know that the skills they have acquired are not either salable or useful in their native lands. Those who return home often become disillusioned, eventually emigrate, or become academics in their native land, where they can transmit their irrelevant knowledge to others.

It is not possible to teach others to develop themselves, nor can we show them how to do so. One cannot learn how to play a piano by attending lectures or watching others play. One can only learn by practice. If one practices, then watching and listening to others can help. Learning how to develop, like learning how to play the piano, requires trying, failing over and over again, and eventually succeeding. The role of the "teacher" should be that of giving others an opportunity to learn by practice, encouraging them to do so, supporting them when they fail, recognizing success when it occurs, and offering to try to provide whatever type of assistance they request.

Leadership Defined

The transformation of a static society into one that aggressively pursues development, however well developed it is initially, requires transformational leadership. Such leadership is rare. Despite a large and growing literature dealing with leadership, no significant increase in either the quantity or the quality of leaders has occurred. Nor has the growing literature on transforming society and organizations produced a significant increase in transformations. To a large extent, these failures are due to the ambiguity associated with both concepts, leadership and transformation. Transformation will be defined and contrasted with reform in the last section of this chapter. Here we define leadership.

Because the terms *administration*, *management*, and *leadership* are often used interchangeably, important differences between them are concealed. As a result, managers are frequently mistaken for leaders, and administrators for managers. The meanings we attribute to these terms are as follows:

Administration consists of directing others in the pursuit of ends by using means, both ends and means having been specified by a third party.

Management consists of directing others in the pursuit of ends by using means, both ends and means having been selected by the manager. (Executives are managers who manage other managers.)

Leadership consists of encouraging and facilitating others both in the pursuit of ends and in the use of means that they have either selected or approved.

So defined, leadership requires an ability to bring the will and desires of followers into consonance with those of the leader so they follow that leader voluntarily, and with enthusiasm and dedication. Voluntarism, enthusiasm, and dedication are not necessarily involved in compliance with the will of either a manager or an administrator. But these attributes are needed for transformations.

The Creation of Visions

Leadership . . . has two main functions. One is to see the vision and develop the strategies that lead towards it. . . . That vision has to be jointly formulated and subscribed to by the heads of the different units. The other is to create an environment which makes it possible to implement the strategies. (Carlzon 1990–91)

A vision is an image of a system that is considered to be significantly more desirable than the existing system. A transforming vision is one that cannot be realized without a fundamental change of direction, which for society involves a change of the status quo, a change in the distribution of power. It takes courage to lead such a change and to follow its leader. The creation of followers requires more than persuasion; it requires the ability to inspire. Unlike persuasion, inspiration evokes a willingness to make sacrifices in the pursuit of long-run objectives or ideals. So visions that induce their pursuit must be inspiring. An inspiring vision is the product of a creative act, of design. *A transforming vision is a work of art.*

Leadership also requires the ability to guide pursuit of the vision. Inspiration without implementation is provocation, not leadership. Implementation without inspiration is management or administration, also not leadership. Leaders must be creative, or use the creativity of others, in order to inspire, and at the same time be courageous, in order to induce implementation.

An inspiring, courage-evoking vision requires a mobilizing idea, a vision of an ideal such as omnicompetence. "Man has been able to grow enthusiastic over his vision of . . . convincing enterprises. He had put himself to work for the sake of an idea, seeking by magnificent exertions to arrive at the incredible. And in the end, he has arrived there" (Jose Ortega y Gasset 1966, p. 1).

Visions may consist of either positive or negative images. Positive images incorporate something that we do not have but want, for example, law and order, a clean and healthy environment, and peace. Negative images incorporate something that we have but do not want, for example, crime, poverty, a disease, or an enemy. Negative images are much easier to formulate and are easier to use in mobilizing people. However, they are often counterproductive, resulting in outcomes that are less desirable than the one we are trying to get rid of. When, for example, the United States tried to get rid of alcoholism by prohibition, it got rid of neither alcoholism nor alcohol but got organized crime as well. We try to get rid of criminals by incarcerating them, although many studies show that the likelihood of a crime being committed by those released from prison is higher than that of criminals who have not been imprisoned (see Chapter 7).

Idealized designs (as described in Chapter 1) can produce positive visions that in turn can mobilize transformations. In this process those who formulate the design begin by assuming that the system being redesigned was completely destroyed last night, but its environment remains as it was. Then they try to design that system with which they would replace the existing system right now, not at some future time, if they were free to replace it with any system they wanted. It takes courage to destroy an existing system, even if only in the imagination. But such courage is required of leadership.

Summarizing this much then: a transformational leader is one who can formulate or facilitate the formulation of an inspiring vision of something to be sought, something continuously approachable even if unattainable. The leader must also be able to encourage and facilitate pursuit of the vision, by invoking the courage required to do so, even when short-term sacrifices are required, and by making that pursuit fun as well as fulfilling.

Leading Transformations

Bringing about a transformation is not easy. Clearly, the issue of leadership is paramount, regardless of where in the organization, government, or community the leadership is located. But there are some characteristics of leadership that are essential to leading a transformation.

THE LEADER AS A ROLE MODEL

If a person wants others to follow her or his leadership, then the leader must be a role model that others want to emulate. The essential ingredient here is this: do not ask others to do something you (the leader) would not do. Regardless of how onerous, difficult, tedious, or even hazardous the task might be, if the leader is not willing to do it, others ought not to be asked to do so. People will be much more willing to follow a leader when they know they will not be asked to do something the leader would not do. The Mantua transformation discussed above is a classic example of this type of leadership. Herman Wrice did everything that he asked others in the community to do, and he was more exposed to danger than was anyone else. He persisted even after his home was looted and his automobile was destroyed several times, and he received a number of threats to his life.

KNOWING WHAT NOT TO DO

Abandonment is the term Peter Drucker uses to describe the process of not continuing to do things when they no longer add value, even though they may be time-honored, traditional, or otherwise considered sacrosanct (Drucker 1974, pp. 93–94). Simply doing things because they have always been done is contrary to transformational leadership. The transformational leader understands that planning entails the discarding of the old as well as adding the new.

There are seldom enough resources to do everything we might like to do. This means that choices must be made about the use of resources. In making these choices, the transformational leader thinks about what adds value and what doesn't and what contributes to development and what doesn't. Courage is required to make such choices when they are not popular.

RECOGNIZING WHEN THE EMPEROR
DOESN'T HAVE NEW CLOTHES

We live in a society that seeks instantaneous gratification and a constant flow of the new. This is why we flit from one fad to another in government, organizations, entertainment, fashion, and the media. Stories stay in newspapers or on television, for example, only as long as they sell newspapers or attract viewers, typically twenty-four hours; few issues are covered in depth and few media carry those that are. Moreover, the desire for the new and the magic bullet that will solve our problems leads people to see change where it really doesn't exist. Much of what is touted as change is nothing more than applying a new name to something that has been going on all along. In organizations, for example, redesign is now called *restructuring*; firing or laying off employees is now labeled *rightsizing* or *downsizing*; comparative evaluation is now referred to as *benchmarking*; and *immediately* is now *real time*.

Transformations take time; they have to be pursed rigorously and in depth. The direction of a transformation should not be set in stone; it can and should change when events and new information so indicate. At the same time, a transformation should not be subject to the whims and fads that are so much a part of our society. And this is another characteristic of the transformational leader: the ability to distinguish between real change and fad, between semantics and substance—that is, to know when the emperor's clothes are new and when they are not.

WHY LEADERSHIP CANNOT BE TAUGHT

Teaching cannot produce great leaders, precisely because leadership is essentially an aesthetic activity. Tools and techniques usable in creative work are the most that can be taught, but not creativity. One can be taught to draw, sculpt, compose, and write better than one would otherwise, but one cannot be taught to do so creatively with excellence, to be an artist.

In school, students are taught to seek solutions that their teachers expect; student success depends on it. This even carries over to corporate and government managers who, when presented with a problem, want to know what kind of solution their bosses expect. This approach precludes creativity, because creativity is the production of solutions that are not expected. Transformational leaders are driven by ideas, not by the expectations of others. They are skillful at beating the system, not at submitting to it.

Leadership is much more an art than a science. If it were a matter of learning a specific method or technique and applying it, a surplus of leaders would be available. Leadership is an ability which, if present, can be developed through experience, but neither the ability nor the experience can be taught. But leadership-expanding experience can be gained. In order to develop leaders, opportunities for developmental experiences should be provided. This means that people must have the opportunity to fail as well as succeed, because, as we noted in Chapter 5, without failure there is no learning, and without learning there is no development.

Why leadership cannot be taught is revealed in the following story:

> A highly regarded leader was asked to what he attributed his success; he replied that it was due to making good decisions. He was then asked what was the basis of his making good decisions. He replied, "Experience." He was then asked how he got the required experience. He replied, "By making bad decisions."

Systemic Transformations

A system is transformed, as contrasted with reformed, when its structure or functions are changed fundamentally. Such changes are discontinuous and qualitative, quantum leaps. For example, Ghandi led the transformation of India from a colonial state to an independent democracy. In contrast, Roosevelt reformed the United States; all of the changes he brought about were within the existing system of government.

Reform maintains the existing system but modifies its behavior; it manipulates the system's efficiency with respect to the same objectives as it had previously. Transformation involves changes of ends as well as means. Reform is preoccupied with *doing things right*, even the wrong things. Transformation is concerned with *doing the right things*, as well as doing them right. Put another way: when a system is reformed, the way it is conceptualized, thought of—for example, as an organism—is not changed. When it is transformed, the way it is conceptualized is changed—for example, from an organism to a social system.

In a society conceptualized as an organism, as most are (see Chapter 7), the government is not thought of as an instrument of its parts. "Ask not what the government can do for you but what you can do for the government." The parts are thought of as instruments of the whole.

"Theirs is not to question why; theirs is just to do or die." In contrast, when a society is conceptualized as a social system, service to its parts, its stakeholders, is its principal function. Those who govern and lead are taken to be public servants in fact as well as in word. In a reformed society, the leader is one who empowers the followers. In a transformed society, the leader is one who is empowered by the followers.

Epilogue: How to Get Started

The designs presented in this book involve radical changes of our society; they are intended to *transform*, not merely reform society. It is difficult enough to reform society, that is, change its behavior but leave its structure essentially as is. Transforming society requires fundamental change of both the structure and the functioning of society; it requires a revolution.

Fortunately, not all revolutions need be violent, for example, the Industrial Revolution and now the Postindustrial Revolution. Fundamental change can occur without bloodshed, or at least without much. Recall that even in the Industrial Revolution the Luddites and some others drew some blood. However, when a society considers itself successful, as ours does, there is virtually no incentive to engage in a transformation. To quote Peter Drucker, "He whom the Gods would destroy they first give forty years of success."

Strong and visionary leadership can initiate transformation. Ataturk brought about fundamental progressive changes in Turkey. Transformation is currently occurring in Russia. Must we sit on our hands, and brain, waiting for visionary and mobilizing leadership? Fortunately, there are examples of societal transformations, and not all of them occurred as a result of inspiring leadership *from the top* of the organization involved. The leadership often came from lower down in the organization.

Most of the examples of transformations of social systems are found in corporations which, more than any other type of organization in our society, are forced to compete effectively in order to survive, let alone thrive. There are corporations like Gortech, Westinghouse Furniture Systems, Herman Miller, SAS, and Federal Express that have converted from hierarchical bureaucratic organizations into lowerarchical task-oriented communities.

Many corporate transformations have begun in a part of an organization and spread to other parts contagiously. For example, a revolution was initiated at Kodak by a sixth-level manager, Henry Pfendt. A part of an organization can transform itself without the whole organization changing. This happened at the Tennessee Operations of Alcoa as a result of the leadership of Richard Ray, who managed it.

Systemic transformations are not restricted to corporations. Schools have effected transformations—for example, the Sudbury Valley School in Framingham, Massachusetts, under the leadership of Daniel Greenberg; the Dental School at the University of Kentucky; and the Social Systems Sciences Department in the Wharton School of the University of Pennsylvania.

The best place to start a revolution is where you are!

Nothing leads to the failure of social systems like success; it brings complacency and conservatism. It is equally true that nothing induces fundamental systemic changes more than successful systemic changes. This means wherever you are in a social system, you can get things started, but not necessarily without risk. Transformations, revolutions, are seldom risk-free, but few things worth pursuing are risk-free.

All aspects of our design are possible, but we do not pretend that they are politically feasible. However, the principal obstructions to feasibility are in people's minds as self-imposed constraints. Statements such as "That will never work" and "We haven't done it that way before" more often than not are unfounded but are used as reasons not to do something, particularly something different. As the cartoon philosopher Pogo said, "We have met the enemy, and he is us." Recognition of these self-imposed constraints enables us to realize a much closer approximation to an idealized design than we could otherwise.

Appendix: A Way of Resolving Conflict

Assuming two individuals or groups (A and B) are in disagreement, the procedure involves the following steps.

> *1. A listens to B express B's views until A feels able to formulate B's position in a way that is acceptable to B. A then attempts to do so. If the effort is unacceptable to B, the effort continues until B accepts A's formulation. Then the roles are reversed.*

If one of the parties wants to maintain a current state—for example, to retain capital punishment—that party should be the first listener. In other words, advocates of change should present their positions first. If one wants to abolish capital punishment and the other wants to maintain it, the advocate of change should present that party's position first and the other restate it to the former's satisfaction. The reason for working in this order is that the one who wants to maintain a current state is less likely to understand the other's position. As the American humorist Ambrose Bierce (1967) observed, "There is but one way to do nothing, but diverse ways of doing something." If both participants seek change, the choice of who comes first should be made by chance.

In some cases this first step may be enough to produce consensus. In others, some or all of the following steps may be required.

*2. Each party formulates the conditions under which that
party believes the position of the other would be valid.*

For example, in a dispute over capital punishment, the one who is opposed to it should state the conditions under which that person believes it would be justified. For example, "I believe capital punishment would be justified if it could be shown that it prevented more capital crimes than there were executions produced by it." Such statements identify "resolving conditions" and make it possible to convert many differences of opinion into questions of fact; for example, does capital punishment reduce the total number of lives lost through murder?

On occasion one party may take the position that the other's position is not justified under any conditions. Then the party that holds the unconditional belief should be called on to propose a method by which two who hold conflicting unconditional beliefs can resolve their differences. If that party can do so, and the method is accepted by the other, the discussion goes on from there. If the method is not accepted by the other, the proposal becomes the issue to be debated and the opponents would return to the first step. If both parties maintain that such a disagreement cannot be resolved, then the discussion is at an end unless they involve a third party who can propose either a method of resolving the difference or a resolution which the parties have agreed to accept before it is revealed. The third party could be a higher-unit leader.

*3. Once the resolving conditions have been agreed to,
each party formulates a concept of how the actual conditions can be determined.*

The parties might agree on these conditions. Returning to the previous example involving capital punishment, they might agree to obtain data from states in each of the four classes shown in Table 2.2. They might also agree that if the average percentage increase in capital crimes per year in states that changed from no capital punishment to its use is less than the corresponding average in each of the other three categories, then capital punishment is an effective deterrent to capital crimes.

If the parties cannot agree on how to determine the match between actual and resolving conditions, they should take this disagreement as the issue and return to the first step. Then they should proceed through the successive steps until this issue is resolved. Once this issue is resolved, they can return to the point at which they broke off.

> *4. Once agreement on how to establish the relevant conditions has been reached, the parties attempt to determine what these conditions actually are, that is, conduct the test.*

Presumably, this test would settle the issue. If such a determination is neither possible nor feasible, the parties can proceed to the next step.

> *5. A table is prepared in which the different positions being argued form the rows, and the justifying conditions of each form the columns.*

Such a table for the capital-punishment debate is shown in Figure 2.2.

> *6. Now each party decides independently for each position what is the most serious error that could be made. Then, if the parties agree on the relative seriousness of the errors, the position with the least possible maximum error is selected. If they do not agree, this becomes the issue that should be taken back to the first step.*

The procedure described here requires more control of the discussion of an issue than the opposing parties themselves can normally provide. Therefore, an impartial facilitator acceptable to both parties is usually required.

In some cases there is not enough time to uncover the underlying factual disagreement, or to design and conduct an acceptable test that would not be too costly. When it is apparent that consensus cannot be reached through discussion and a test is not feasible or practical, the leader of the unit can employ the following procedure in a meeting of all the participants in the decision process. Once it is apparent that agreement is not being reached, the leader asks participants to summarize their position succinctly. Then the leader reveals what he or she would do if given the choice. However, the leader makes it clear that if the others reach an agreement, even if it differs from the leader's position on the issue, the leader would accept it and act accordingly. Finally, the leader goes around the room once again asking for each participant's opinion. If two or more participants disagree, then, in effect, they agree on the leader's choice. If they all agree with one another, regardless of what the leader prefers, their agreement becomes the basis of action.

References

Ackoff, Russell L. 1974. *Redesigning the future*. New York: Wiley.

Adams, Carolyn Teich. 1986. Homelessness in the postindustrial city. *Urban Affairs Quarterly* 21 (June): 531.

Bierce, Ambrose. 1967. *The enlarged devil's dictionary*. Harmondsworth, Middlesex, England: Penguin Books.

Burt, M. R., et al. 2001. *Helping America's homeless*. Washington, D.C.: Urban Institute Press.

Business Week. 1983. Why Washington likes consumption taxes. June 13, p. 80.

Carlzon, Jan. 1990–91. Putting people on the freedom framework. *Business Strategy International* 1, no. 33 (winter): 53f.

Daedalus. 1994. Health and wealth. (Fall).

The Economist. 1997. Education and the wealth of nations, March 29, p. 15.

Drucker, Peter F. 1974. *Management: Tasks, responsibilities, practices*. New York: Harper and Row.

Edwards, Carolyn, Lella Gandini, and George Forman, eds. 1995. *The hundred languages of children: The Reggio Emilia approach to early childhood education*. Norwood, N.J.: Ablex.

Ellwood, David T. 1994. Reducing poverty by replacing welfare. In *Welfare realities*, ed. May Jo Bane and David T. Ellwood. Cambridge: Harvard University Press.

Farnsworth, Clyde H. 1997. The penal colony learned a lesson. *New York Times*, August 10, p. E6.

Greenberg, Daniel. 2000. *A clearer view: New insights into the Sudbury School model*. Framingham, Mass.: The Sudbury School Press, no. 105.

Handy, C. 1999. *Waiting for the mountain to move*. San Francisco: Jossey-Bass.

Henry, Jules. 1965. *Culture against man*. New York: Vintage Books.

Howard, Ronald A. 1967. Free for all. *Management Science* 13: B-681–85.

Jencks, Christopher. 1970. Giving money for schooling: Educational vouchers. *Phi Delta Kappa* (September): 49–52.

———. *The homeless*. 1994. Cambridge: Harvard University Press.

Kozol, Jonathan. 1995. *Amazing grace*. New York: Crown.

Laing, R. D. 1967. *The politics of experience*. New York: Pantheon.

Link, B., et al. 1995. Lifetime and five-year prevalence of homelessness in the United States. *American Journal of Orthopsychiatry* 65(3): 347–54.

Lasch, Christopher. 1972. Toward a theory of post-industrial society. In *Politics in the post-welfare state*, ed. M. Donald Hancock and Gideon Sjoberg. New York: Columbia University Press.

Mathews, Jessica. 1996. Social Security's scary demographics. *Philadelphia Inquirer*, January 9, p. A11.

Ortega y Gasset, Jose. 1966. *Mission of the university*. New York: Norton.

Rapoport, Anatol. 1960. *Fights, games, and debates*. Ann Arbor: University of Michigan Press.

Rovin, Sheldon, Neville Jeharajah, et al. 1994. *An idealized design of the U.S. healthcare system*. Bala Cynwyd, Pa.: Interact.

Rubin, Trudy. 1997. Arafat's autocratic ways hurt Palestinians and the peace process. *Philadelphia Inquirer*, December 24, p. A11.

Snow, David A., et al. 1986. The myth of pervasive mental illness among the homeless. *Social Problems* 33 (June): 407–23.

Skeel, David, and William Stuntz. 2002. Another attempt to legislate corporate honesty. *New York Times*, July 10, p. 21.

Warwick, David R. 1992. The cash-free society. *The Futurist* (November-December): 19–22.

Weidenbaum, Murray. 1992, July. The case for taxing consumption. *Contemporary Issue Series 54*. St. Louis: Center for the Study of American Business, Washington University.

World Health Organization (WHO). 2000. *World Health Report 2000*. Geneva: WHO.

The Wrice Process. 1993. Philadelphia: Anti-Drug Coalition and Pennsylvania Office of the Attorney General.

Wylie, Ann. 1993. Putting prisoners to work. *Lafayette Magazine* (summer): 27–29.

Index

Illustrations are referenced by *italic* page numbers.

abandonment, 161
abortion, 17, 30, 138
absolution of problems, 9, 10, 92
Ackoff, Russell L., 39
Adams, Carolyn Teich, 117
Adams, Forrest, 155
administration vs. leadership, 158
adoption, 119
aesthetics and development, 151–52
Afghanistan, 145, 146
aged persons. *See* elderly persons
Alcoa, 166
alcohol and drug use: crime, drug
    abuse as, 126; development, 156,
    157; legalization of drugs, 121,
    135–36; prohibition, unintended
    results of, 98, 134, 136, 160; sin
    taxes on alcohol, 135; teenage
    drinking, causes of, 111; welfare,
    117, 121
American Association of Boarding
    Schools, 120

analysis vs. synthesis, 2–4
Anderson (corporation), 142
Anheuser-Busch, 111
apprenticeships, 90
Arthur Andersen Company, 143
Ataturk, Kemal, 165
authority in governance, 19–20
automobiles, 55–58

Barry, Marion, 139
Bierce, Ambrose, 124, 167
biological vs. social systems, 8, 141,
    163–64
block as basic unit of cities, 44–46,
    45, 47, 48
blue laws (Sundays, laws applicable
    to), 126, 134
BMW, 58
boarding schools, 119–20
bottom-up vs. top-down, 19, 27,
    165–66
budgeting. *See* costs and savings

bureaucracy, reducing, 31–33
Burt, Martha R., 114
Busch Research Center, Wharton
    School, University of Pennsylvania,
    155–56
buses, 55
Bush, George H. W., 124

campaigning for office, 26
capital punishment, 29–30, *31*, 168
cars, *55–58*
case studies, 94
cash-free society, 147
change: education preparing for, 86,
    109; leadership's ability to distin-
    guish real change from fads, 161–
    62; primary health care providers,
    66–67; transformation vs. refor-
    mation, 62, 163–64, 165
children and minors: abuse of, 120;
    child support, child care, and foster
    care, 111, 118–20; criminals, juve-
    nile and young adult, 125, 131–
    32; discussion or treatment of
    problems regarded as encourage-
    ment of dysfunctional behavior,
    111; divorce from parents, 120;
    parents, minor children as, 119,
    120. *See also* education
cities, 39–51; block as basic unit of,
    44–46, *45*, *47*, *48*; design pro-
    posal, 44–51; design requirements,
    41–43; districts, 49; education and
    schools, 46–48, 52; environmental
    concerns, 43, 61; equal opportu-
    nity and access, 42; flexibility, im-
    portance of, 61; fractal design, *45*;
    governance, 40, 61; heterogeneous,
    41–42; homelessness, 117; housing
    deterioration, preventing, 52; land
    ownership in, 51; layouts for, 49–

51, *50*; minorities and disadvan-
    taged, 40–42; neighborhoods, 46–
    49; proximity and transportation
    issues, 42–43; public open space,
    43, 44; redesign requirements, 41–
    43; sections, 49; units of, 44–49
clinical or therapeutic treatment of
    crime, 127, 129
clockwork, universe as, 2–3
collective authority, 19
committees-of-the-whole, 20
communities: cities, 46–49, 61; cor-
    porations treated as, 143; develop-
    ment aid, 154–56; education, 46–
    48, 52, 106, *107*; elderly and dis-
    abled persons, 120; governance, 8,
    20–25; health care boards, 69–74;
    homelessness, 117–18; new hous-
    ing, 53; policing, 132–33; prisons
    as correctional communities, 128–
    30; transport, community-owned,
    55; work, welfare, and workfare,
    113, 122
Community for Creative Non-
    violence, 115
community health care boards, 69–74
complex problems and systems
    (messes), 83, 95, 97–98, 108, 110
computer-assisted learning, 84–85,
    87–88, *89*, 92
computer technology, crime based on,
    126
conflict resolution, 28–30, 167–70
consensus vs. minority/majority deci-
    sionmaking, 17–18, 28–30, 167–
    70
consumption taxes, 33–36
contraction/growth vs. decline/
    development, 150
controlling or deterrent treatment of
    crime, 127

corporate crime, 142–44
corporate redesign history, 166
corruption, 138–44; causes of, 140–41; corporate crime, 142–44; defined, 139; measures for reducing, 142; public tolerance of, 139–40
costs and savings: education, 102–4, 105; governmental budgets, 27–28; health care, 62–63, 80, 97–98; transportation, 58; work, welfare, and workfare, 112–13
courts, function of, 137–38
creativity, importance of, xii; development, 152; education, 83–85; vision and leadership, 159–60
crime and punishment, 29–30, 31, 124–49, 168; cash-free society, 147; causes of crime, 124–25; clinical or therapeutic treatment, 127, 129; corporate crime, 142–44; corruption, 138–44; courts and judiciary, function of, 137–38; danger, criminals not posing, 131–32; danger to others, persons posing, 128–30; definition of crime, 125–26; deterrent or controlling treatment, 127; development, problems associated with, 157; drug abuse as crime, 126; drugs, legalization of, 121, 135–36; law, 126, 134–36; opportunity vs. problem, crime as, 125; parental responsibility for young offenders, 125, 131–32; police, 132–33; prohibition, unintended results of, 2, 98, 134, 160; property or freedom of others, persons taking, 130; psychological treatment, 127, 129; rates of crime, 124; recidivism, prisons, and incarceration, 2, 124–25, 160; restitution, 127, 130, 131, 132, 147–48;

retribution, 124–25, 147–48; social environment, offenders causing harm to, 131; social failure, crime as, 125, 134, 149; supportive or protecting treatment, 127; terrorism, 144–47; treatment vs. punishment, 125, 130; types of criminals, 126–27; types of treatment, 127; victimless crimes, 126; work for prisoners, 128–29, 130; work-release programs, 130; young/juvenile offenders, 125, 131–32. See also corruption; prisons and incarceration; terrorism; victims of crime; capital punishment
crusades, 153
culture, 8

dangerous offenders, 128–30
data/information vs. knowledge/understanding/wisdom, 98–99
day care, 119–20
death penalty (capital punishment), 29–30, 31, 168
decline/development vs. contraction/growth, 150
defense as governmental function, 30–31
democratic government. See governance
demographic change: governance affected by, 16–17; homelessness, 117
depreciation of housing, taxation of, 51–52
Descartes, René, 2
desires: importance of fulfilling (vs. getting rid of what we do not want), 2, 63, 153; needs vs., 151
deterioration of housing, taxation of, 51–52

deterrent or controlling treatment of
crime, 127
development, 150–68; aesthetics and,
151–52; aspects and pursuits
required for, 151–52; communities, aid for, 154–56; creativity,
importance of, 152; defined, 150–
51; education, 146, 153–54; external aid for, 154–56; growth vs., 8,
150–51; ideas vs. ideologies, 153–
54; leadership and, 152, 162–63;
Mantua, Philadelphia, 146, 149,
155–56, 161; omnicompetence as
limit of, 152; stimulating, 152–53;
terrorism, 154; underdeveloped
countries, application of development principles to, 157–58
disabled persons, 111, 117, 120
disadvantaged persons. *See* minorities
and disadvantaged
discrimination: cities, 40–42; crime as
social failure, 125; governance,
17–18; welfare, 122
discussion as learning method (seminars), 89–90
dissolution of problems, 10–11, 92–
93
districts of cities, 49
"do anything not restricting others"
principle of government, 19
doughnut cities, 40
draft laws, Vietnam era, 134
Drucker, Peter, 1, 161, 165
drugs and alcohol. *See* alcohol and
drug use
Dukakis, Michael, 124

economics. *See* costs and savings
education, 82–109; boarding schools
for children in care of state, 119–
20; case studies, 94; change, preparing for, 86, 109; city/commu-
nity schools, 46–48, 52; complex
problems and systems (messes), 83,
95, 97–98, 108; computer-assisted
learning, 84–85, 87–88, 89, 92;
content, 84–85, 92–93; costs and
savings, 102–4, 105; creativity, importance of, 83–85; data/informa-
tion vs. knowledge/ understanding/
wisdom, 98–99; development,
146, 153–54; disciplines and departments, 95–97; discussion as
learning method (seminars), 89–
90; errors and mistakes, 99–101;
evaluation and testing of students,
101–2; evaluation of teachers,
105–6; facilities, 46–48, 106, *107*;
forecasts, 100–101; governance,
20; health care providers, 67;
homelessness, 116–17; ideas vs.
ideologies, 153–54; implementing
redesigns, 165–66; independent
learning, 91–92; intransigents,
118; leadership, 162–63; learning
vs. being taught, 84–87; lectures,
92; modular/pre-fabricated structures, 53, 60–61; practical instruction, 91; problem-solving, 88, 92–
98; public vs. private, 102–4;
questions, exercises, and problems,
93–95; redesign proposal, 85–86;
Reggio Emilia schools, Italy, 91,
92, 106, 119; research cells,
practicums, and apprenticeships,
90; scheduling and school years,
107–8, *108*; single vs. varied curriculum and pedagogy, 84–85, 92;
social function of, 83–84, 91; systems thinking and systematic redesign, 83, 108; teachers, faculty,
and staff, 86–87, 104–6; teaching

vs. being taught, 86–87; terrorism, 146, 154; trimesters, 107–8, *108*; unlearning irrelevant information, 85; value of what is learned, assessing, 99; vouchers, 52, 102–4; and welfare, and poverty, 114

effectiveness vs. efficiency, 1

Einstein, Albert, xi, 8

elderly persons: child care, 119; homelessness, 117; public benefits for, 120–21; skills registry for, 120–21; social security benefits, 121–22

elections and voting, 25–26; corruption, 139; immigration/emigration, 24–25; multiple votes in relevant governmental units, 22–23; participation in, 14, 25–26; problems with current system, 15–16; *Someone Else* voting option, 25

electric-powered vehicles, 58

Ellwood, David, 113

emigration/immigration, 24–25, 64

employers and employees: corporate crime, 140–42; corporate redesign history, 166; health care, 64–65, 80; travel to work, tax on distance of, 54

Enron, 142

environmental concerns: cities, 43, 61; employment tax on distance employees must travel to work, 54; public open space, 43, 44, 53; solar power, 52, 58; transportation, 58, 61

equality of opportunity, 42, 122–23

errors, learning from, 99–101

evaluation and testing of students, 101–2

evaluation of teachers, 105–6

examinations as educational tools, 101–2

exercises, questions, and problems, 93–95

expressways, 54

extended health care units, 77–78

extroverted fundamentalism, 145

fact, design decisions reached by tests of, 29–30, *31*, 168–69

faculty and staff, 86, 87, 104–6

families: criminals, juvenile and young adult, 125, 131–32; indigent, support for, 111, 117; single-parent families, 117, 120. *See also* children and minors

Family School, Philadelphia, 119

Federal Express, 166

Federal Reserve Bank, 97

Feldstein, Martin S., 34

finances. *See* costs and savings

Ford, 58

forecasts as educational tool, 100–101

foster care, 111, 118–20

fractal design of cities, *45*

France, "Tulip" transportation system, 58

freight transportation, 59–61

fundamentalist thinking, 144–45, 154

Gall, John, 1

gambling, 126, 135

gangs, 156

General Motors, 58

ghettoes and slums, 40, 41

Girard College, 120

Gortech, 166

governance, 14–38; authority, 19–20; bureaucracy, monopolies, and subsidized services, 31–33; cities, 40, 61; corruption, 139; definition of democracy, 18–19; demographic change, effect of, 16–17; education, 20; legislative support system, 36–37; majority/minority vs. consensus decisionmaking, 17–18, 28–30; military and defense, 30–31; minorities and disadvantaged, representation of, 15, 17; operations and function of government units, 27–28; participative democracy as principle value of, 14–15, 18; redesign proposal, 20–37; redesign requirements, 19–20; representation and misrepresentation, 15–18; structure of government, 20–25, 23; taxation, 33–36; units of government, 20–24, 23, 27–28. *See also* elections and voting

green space, 43, 44, 53

Greenberg, Daniel, 166

growth vs. development, 8, 150–51

Hawken School, Cleveland, 88

Head Start, 119

health care, 62–81; 1994 U.S. health care reform proposals, 62, 81; beneficiaries of system, 64; community boards, 69–74; complexity of problem, 97–98; costs and savings, 62–63, 80, 97–98; crime, clinical or therapeutic treatment of, 127, 129; education of providers, 67; employers and employees, 64–65, 80; extended care units, 77–78; insurance for health care providers, 67–68; lack of coverage under current system, 62, 80–81; levels of care, 74–78; malls, 78, 79; malpractice insurance, 67–68; modular/pre-fabricated structures, 53, 60–61; nurse-practitioners, 75; outside-the-system primary care

providers, 67; primary care, 65–69, 74–75; problem patients, 68–69; redesign proposal, 64–81; secondary, tertiary, and quaternary care units, 76–77; taxation, 64–65; units, 74–78, 75; vouchers, 64–65; wellness subsystem, 74, 78–80, 79; women's primary care, 75. *See also* primary care providers

Henry, Jules, 83–84

Herbert, George, 110

Herman Miller, 166

heterogeneous cities, 41–42

hierarchy vs. lowerarchy. *See* lowerarchy vs. hierarchy

homelessness, 114–18, 123

Honda, 58

housing, 51–54; deterioration, preventing, 51–52; homelessness, 117; modular/pre-fabricated, 53, 60; new housing, 52–53; property tax, 2, 51–52; right to acceptable housing, 53–54; town and row houses, 52

Howard, Ronald A., 134

Hun School, 120

idealized design/redesign, 11–13, 160

ideas vs. ideologies, 153–54

illiteracy, 114

immigration/emigration, 24–25, 64

incarceration. *See* prisons and incarceration

income insurance for health care providers, 68

independent learning, 91–92

Industrial Revolution, 3, 39, 165

information/data vs. knowledge/ understanding/wisdom, 98–99

insecurity as cause of corruption, 141

institutionalization, 111, 117
insurance for health care providers,
    67–68
interaction of societal parts, 3–7
intransigents, 117, 118
introverted fundamentalism, 145
Iranian tobacco laws, 135
Iraq, 145
Israeli-Palestinian conflict, 140, 145
Italy, Reggio Emilia region schools,
    91, 92, 106, 119

Jencks, Christopher, 102, 115
joining new governmental units, 24
judiciary, function of, 137–38
justice system. See crime and punish-
    ment

KA vehicle (Ford), 58
Kaleidoscope program, 119
knowledge/understanding/wisdom vs.
    data/information, 98–99
Kodak, 166
Kuttab, Daoud, 140

Laing, Ronald, 42, 84
land. See real estate
law, crime, and punishment, 126,
    134–36
Lawrenceville, 120
leadership, 158–63; choices, making,
    161; defining leadership, 158–59;
    development, 152, 162–63; educa-
    tion, 162–63; real change from,
    distinguishing, 161–62; role mod-
    els, 161; transformational leaders,
    160–63; vision, creating, 159–60
Lebanon, 146
lectures as educational means, 92
legislative support system, 36–37
Libya, 145

literacy programs, 114
lotteries, 135
lowerarchy vs. hierarchy, 165–66;
    cities, 44; community health care
    boards, 70–71; corporations, 141;
    governance, 19, 27
Luddites, 165

majority/minority vs. consensus
    decisionmaking, 17–18, 28–30,
    167–70
malpractice insurance for health care
    providers, 67–68
management vs. leadership, 158
Mantua, Philadelphia development
    project, 146, 149, 155–56, 161
mass transit, 55, 58
mechanical or biological vs. social sys-
    tems, 8, 141, 163–64
mechanistic view of universe, 2–3
medical care. See health care
Medicare and Medicaid, 80
Meese, Edwin, 116
Mercedes, 58
messes (complex problems and sys-
    tems), 83, 95, 97–98, 108, 110
Middle East conflict, 145–46
military, 30–31, 134
minorities and disadvantaged: cities,
    40–42; crime as social failure, 125;
    governmental representation of,
    15, 17; homelessness, 114–18;
    poverty, causes of, 112; welfare,
    115–16, 122–23
minority/majority vs. consensus
    decisionmaking, 17–18, 28–30,
    167–70
minors. See children and minors
misrepresentation in government,
    15–18
mistakes, learning from, 99–101

modular/pre-fabricated structures, 53, 60–61
monopolies in government, reducing, 31–33
motor vehicles, private, 55–58
multiple votes in relevant governmental units, 22–23

National Rifle Association, 17
needs and wants: desires vs. needs, 151; importance of fulfilling, 2, 63, 153
neighborhoods in cities, 46–49
Newton, Isaac, 2, 3
nurse-practitioners, 75

Oak Lane Country Day School, Philadelphia, 87
older persons. *See* elderly persons
omnicompetence as limit of development, 152
open space, public, 43, 44, 53
opportunity: crime as, 125; equality of, 42, 122–23; problems as opportunities, 9, 125

Palestine, 140, 145
parental responsibility for juvenile and young adult criminals, 125, 131–32
parks in cities, 43, 44
party politics, 26
pedagogy. *See* education
Pfendt, Henry, 166
piecemeal improvements, 2
Pogo, 166
police, 132–33
political parties, 26
Postindustrial Revolution, 165
poverty, 110–12, 122–23, 125. *See also* welfare

practicums, 90
pre-fabricated/modular structures, 53, 60–61
preventive policing, 132–33
primary health care, 65–69, 74–75
primary health care providers, 65–69; changing, 66–67; education, 67; income insurance, 68; malpractice insurance, 67–68; outside the system, 67; problem patients, 68–69; services provided by, 66
prisons and incarceration, 127; commission of crimes within prisons, 129; danger to others, persons posing, 128–30; recidivism, 2, 124–25, 160. *See also* crime and punishment
private education, 102–4
private motor vehicles, 55–58
private services vs. public services, 30–33
problems and problem-solving: absolution, solution, resolution, and dissolution, 9, 10–11, 92, 93; complex problems and systems (messes), 83, 95, 97–98, 108, 110; computer-assisted learning, 88; crime and punishment as opportunity vs. problem, 125; definition and treatment of, 9–11, 92–95; disciplines and departments, academic, 95–97; discussion or treatment regarded as encouragement of dysfunctional behavior, 111; education, 88, 92–98; exercises and questions, 93–95; opportunities, problems as, 9, 125
prohibition, unintended results of, 2, 98, 134, 136, 160
property tax, 2, 51–52
prostitution, 126

protecting or supportive treatment of
    crime, 127
psychological treatment of crime, 127,
    129
public education, 102–4
public open space, 43, 44, 53
public transportation, 55, 58
public vs. private services, 30–33
public works army, 118
punishment of crimes. *See* crime and
    punishment

quaternary health care units, 76–77
questions, exercises, and problems,
    93–95

race. *See* discrimination; minorities
    and disadvantaged; segregation
rail transport, 59, 60
Rapaport, Anatole, 30
Ray, Richard, 166
Reagan Administration, 34, 116
real estate. *See also* housing: owner-
    ship of land in cities, 51; property
    tax, 2, 51–52
recidivism, 2, 124–25, 160
redesigning society, 9, 10–11, 92, 93;
    idealized design/redesign, 11–13,
    160; implementing redesigns, 165–
    66; need for and importance of, xi–
    xiii; principles of, 1–2; proof vs.
    preferences in evaluating redesigns,
    xii; reformation vs. transformation,
    62, 163–64, 165; systems think-
    ing, 2–11. *See also* absolution, so-
    lution, resolution, and dissolution.
Rees, Mary, 87
reformation vs. transformation, 62,
    163–64, 165
Reggio Emilia schools, Italy, 91, 92,
    106, 119

Renaissance, 2
Renault, 58
representation and misrepresentation
    in government, 15–18
research cells, 90
resolution of problems, 9, 10–11, 92,
    93
restitution for crimes, 127, 130, 131,
    132, 147–48
Reston, James, 14
retired persons, 120–21. *See also* eld-
    erly persons
retribution for crime, 124–25, 147–
    48
right thing, importance of doing (vs.
    doing things right), 1, 99, 163
rights: governance, participative
    democracy as principle value of,
    14–15, 18; housing, 53–54
roads and streets, 54
row houses, 52
Russell, Bertrand, 82

SAS, 166
savings estimates. *See* costs and sav-
    ings
scarcity as cause of corruption, 14–
    141
schools. *See* education
secession of governance units, 24
secondary, tertiary, and quaternary
    health care units, 76–77
sections of cities, 49
segregation: cities, 40–42; crime as
    social failure, 125; governance,
    17–18; welfare, 122
self-governing principle, 19
seminars as learning method, 89–90
services, subsidized, 30–33
sexual activity, 111
single-parent families, 117, 120

Sisters of Charity of Nazareth Corporation, 63
skills acquisition and training. *See* education
skills registry for retired persons, 120–21
slums and ghettoes, 40, 41
Snyder, Mitch, 115
social environment, offenders causing harm to, 131
social security benefits, 121–22
social systems: biological or mechanical systems vs., 8, 141, 163–64; corporations as communities, 141; crime as social failure, 125, 134, 149; education, social function of, 83–84, 91; society as social system, 8
sociopaths, 128
solar power, 52, 58
solution of problems, 9–11, 92
Someone Else voting option, 25
special interest groups, 17
Sprowall, Chris, 115
streets and roads, 54
structure of government, 20–25, 23
Stumpfer, Johan, 145
subsidized services, 30–33
substance abuse. *See* alcohol and drug use
suburbs, 40, 61
subways, 55
success, effects of, 165, 166
Sudbury School, Massachusetts, 90, 92
Sufis, 154
Sundays, laws applicable to (blue laws), 126, 134
sunset clause requirements, 136, 148
supportive or protecting treatment of crime, 127

synthetic thinking, development of, 2–4
systems thinking and systematic redesign, 2–11; definition of systems, 4–7; education, 83, 108; interaction of societal parts, 3–7; performance of system as a whole, 6–7; problems, definition and treatment of, 9–11; social system, society as, 8; successful and fundamental systemic changes, 166; synthetic vs. analytical thinking, 2–4; transformation vs. reformation, 163–64

taxation: employment tax on distance employees must travel to work, 54; governance issues, 33–36; health care, 64–65; housing depreciation, 2, 51–52; sin taxes on alcohol and tobacco, 135
taxis, 58
teachers, faculty, and staff, 86–87, 104–6. *See also* education
teenagers. *See* children and minors
terms of office, 26
terrorism, 144–47, 148; computer-assisted, 126; development and, 154; education, 146, 154; fundamentalist thinking, 144–45, 154; responding to, 145–47
tertiary health care units, 76–77
tests as educational tools, 101–2
therapeutic or clinical treatment of crime, 127, 129
threats, problems as, 9
tobacco laws, Iranian, 135
top-down vs. bottom-up, 19, 27, 165–66
town houses, 52
traditional behavior, combating, 161
traffic. *See* transportation

training and skills. *See* education
Trans Ports, 59
transformation vs. reformation, 62,
    163–64, 165
transformational leaders, 160–63
transportation, 54–61; accidents, 57–
    58; cities, 42–43; community-
    owned vehicles, 55; costs and sav-
    ings, 58; employment tax on dis-
    tance employees must travel to
    work, 54; environmental concerns,
    58, 61; expressways, 54; freight,
    59–61; private vehicles and urmo-
    biles, 55–58, 57; public trans-
    portation, 55, 58; streets and
    roads, 54; taxis, 58
trial and error as educational tool,
    99–101
trimester educational schedules, 107–
    8, *108*
trucks, truck drivers, tractors, and
    trailers, 57, 59–61
"Tulip" vehicle system, France, 58
Twain, Mark, 62

underdeveloped countries, application
    of development principles to, 157–
    58
understanding/knowledge/wisdom vs.
    data/information, 98–99
Union of the Homeless, 115
units: cities, 44–49; governance, 20–
    24, *23*, 27–28; health care, 74–78,
    75
University of Kentucky dental school,
    92
University of Pennsylvania, 155–56
urban living. *See* cities
urmobiles, 55–58, 57
utilities, 52–53

values: design evaluation, xii; dis-
    agreements of facts vs. values, 29–
    30, 37, 136; education, 83, 99;
    participative democracy, 14; terror-
    ism, combating, 145
vehicles, private, 55–58
victimless crimes, 126
victims of crime, 132; criminal acts re-
    quiring, 126; restitution, 127, 130,
    131, 132, 147–48
Vietnam era draft laws, 134
voting. *See* elections and voting
vouchers: education, 52, 102–4;
    health care, 64–65

wants and needs: desires vs. needs,
    151; importance of fulfilling (vs.
    getting rid of what we do not
    want), 2, 63, 153
Warwick, David R., 36, 147
Weidenbaum, Murray, 33–34
welfare, 110–23; alcohol and drug
    use, 111, 117, 121; child support,
    child care, and foster care, 111,
    118–20; community basis for, 113,
    122; complex problems and sys-
    tems (messes), 110; costs and sav-
    ings, 112–13; disabled persons,
    111, 117, 120; education, 114; eld-
    erly persons, 117, 119, 120–21;
    family support, 111, 117; home-
    lessness, 114–18, 123; institution-
    alization, 111, 117; intransigents,
    117, 118; minorities and disadvan-
    taged, 115–16, 122–23; poverty,
    110–12, 122–23, 125; social secu-
    rity benefits, 121–22; work and
    workfare, 112–14, 117
wellness health care subsystem, 74,
    78–80, 79
Westinghouse Furniture Systems, 166

Wharton School, University of Pennsylvania, 156
White, Don Anthony, 129
WHO (World Health Organization), 62
Wildavsky, Aaron, 62
Wilde, Oscar, 85
wisdom/understanding/knowledge vs. data/information, 98–99
women's primary health care, 75

work for prison inmatess, 128–29, 130
work-release programs for prison inmates, 130
work, welfare, and workfare, 112–14, 117
World Health Organization (WHO), 62
WorldCom, 142
Wrice, Herman, 155–56, 161